CRAZY
MAN'S
CREEK

CRAZY MAN'S CREEK

by Jack Boudreau

Caitlin Press Inc.

Prince George, BC

1998

Caitlin Press Inc.
Box 2387, Station B
Prince George British Columbia V2N 2S6

Caitlin Press gratefully acknowledges the financial support of the
Canada Council for the Arts for our publishing program. Similarly
we acknowledge the support of the Arts Council of British Columbia.

Layout and design by Eye Design Inc.
Cover design by Terra Firma Graphics
Indexing by Kathy Plett
Photos supplied by Jack Boudreau
Cover photo: Arne Jensen with his favourite horse, Old Madam.

Canadian Cataloguing in Publication Data

Boudreau, Jack 1933–
Crazy Man's Creek

Includes index
ISBN 0-920576-71-0

I. Title
PS8553.O823C72 1998   C813'.54 C98-9102210-6
PR9199.3B618C72 1998

To my parents,
Joe and Bessie Boudreau,
who crossed the Great Divide
in 1969 and 1983 respectively.
Thanks for the love and kindness
and for always being
there for us.

ACKNOWLEDGEMENTS

First, with the deepest respect, I wish to extend gratitude to all the woodsmen who gave freely of their time and memories. Too numerous to give mention to, I can honestly say that they will always hold a special place in my heart.

Next, I wish to thank the *Prince George Citizen* for their permission to reprint; specific credits are given in order.

Also, the Prince George Public Library for the liberal use of their micro-fiche, and for not throwing me out when I appeared there day after day for hours on end.

To Quesnel's *Cariboo Observer* and their magnificent museum, a very special thank you.

Finally, to the individuals who helped and inspired me: many thanks to Maxine Koppe, Josie Haws, Susan Charters, Mary Trick, Ruth Hansen Flynn, Ted and Olive Williams, Harry Weaver, Ben Cook, Gus Lund, Jason Yarmish, Terry Sayce, Glenn Isaac, Paul Paulson, Torsten Berg, and Bob Harkins.

CONTENTS

An editorial for the *Fort George Herald* dated
March 18, 1911, carried an article appropriately
titled "A Romance of the Fur Trade." A brief part
of which follows:

> "...*There is a fatal fascination about the free life
> of the forest that holds a man captive. Such a
> one has heard the call of the wild. To ply the
> paddle, to shoot the wild duck, to hit the trail
> across the frozen bush, to sleep beneath the
> stars, to breathe the scent of cedar or pine –
> these things are life to him whose blood has
> caught the fever...*"

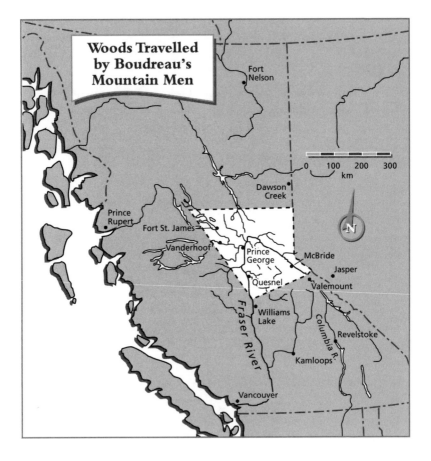

Woods Travelled
by Boudreau's
Mountain Men

INTRODUCTION

A S A LAD, I GREW UP IN A SMALL ISOLATED COMMUNITY with endless mountains for neighbours. The son of a sometimes trapper and full-time woodsman, I took an intense interest in everything to do with nature. When other trappers, guides, or woodsmen visited our home, I was privy to the stories of their adventures in the forests and I hung on their every word. They seemed so utterly fearless—these often bearded men who told stories of remote lakes and mountains, and of grizzly bears that feared nothing. There were wolf packs, 20 or 30 strong, that sometimes followed the men through the forests for miles, their combined howls causing fear even among the bravest of these wilderness wanderers. I had heard the howling of the wolf packs, and even from the safety of our home, they had sent shivers racing along my spine. Sometimes after these men visited, I would lie awake in my bed for hours while visions of mountains full of strange animals raced through my mind.

Many of the stories they told are etched in my memory, among the most precious of my memories because they taught me a love for the forests and mountains that has never faded.

In the 1960s, spurred on by the fact that many of these woodsmen were passing on and taking a great legacy with them, I started writing down these stories and over the next 20 years I visited with many of them to get their stories. Almost all have since passed on, leaving me with the hope that many of fondest memories will live on in these pages.

As I have spent my life in the forests and mountains and have had a great deal to do with animals—especially grizzlies, I was prepared to deal with any exaggerations of sizes and weights, but this never presented itself as a problem. It struck me that these gross exaggerations are more a modern-day phenomena.

Before radios came on the scene, people often spent months in the wilderness living in complete silence; something that is virtually unknown in today's world. I believe this had a direct bearing on the large number of these people who openly talked to themselves. One elderly trapper who spent a great deal of time alone and always maintained a great sense of humour, offered, "Sure I talk to myself; I like to talk to an intelligent man. It's also nice to listen to an intelligent man now and then."

Seriously though, I know from experience that this silence can become so loud that it is deafening, and that it can lead to strange actions: like the hunter who turned to guide Ben Sykes about 1920 and said, "Get me out to civilization at once or you're going to have a crazy man to deal with." This hunter had been raised in New York City and had known only continuous noise. The silence overwhelmed him.

Some of these people were put in a position where they had to become adults at a very young age. Some experienced that special feeling of intense loneliness that one finds only in the wilderness, yet they were barely into their teens. Lawrence Hooker, for example, as a lad of 15, spent 53 days trapping alone in a remote area without seeing another person. He quickly learned that one must plan ahead: like having kindling wood prepared to make a quick fire in the event that he came back to the cabin with near frozen hands or body, or keeping a good supply of wood ahead in case of prolonged sickness. Like many forest wanderers, he knew that the wilderness can be long on beauty and wonder but very short on mercy when an error or foolish act is committed.

Many men paid with their lives for entering a strange area and then getting lost in a blizzard without enough food to see them through. One elderly woodsman told me that he had never been lost in the woods, only turned around a few times. When I asked him what the difference was between the two, he responded, "About one day."

There are stories of hardship and privation, of people who were down but not out; who never lost their sense of humour no matter how bad things got. From the time that prospectors and trappers first visited the interior of the province they have had an endless series of adventures. Fast on their heels, came all the support people, along with the railroad, the sternwheelers, and woodsmen of all types, including a very large number of surveyors to lay out the railway grade and survey the land for the new settlers. The stories in this book make an attempt to include adventures by all of these people and they are not limited to trappers, guides, and prospectors, although they are the main focus.

The first chapter of this book tells of the often overwhelming odds faced by the people moving supplies or their own personal belongings along the Fraser River between Tête Jaune and Fort George, and the staggering loss of life associated with it. I had to include the sternwheelers with the many disasters they faced between Soda Creek and Tête Jaune, because for me they represent the most romantic part of our history. Some stories of events that took place as the railway grade was being constructed are included also.

The effects of the solitude associated with this way of life profoundly changed some of these people. Some became stronger and better people, while others went mad or just kept completely to themselves.

A Dog Team on the Fraser River at Fort George, B. C. No. 105. 1910

Shorty Haynes hauling mail up Fraser to winter camps – 150 miles by dog team in the winter of 1910–11.

All of these types of stories are included, and I ask the reader to bear with me at times as these stories move them rather far from this area.

I have attempted to include interesting adventures of confrontations with wild animals, which were inevitable as people entered more and more into their domains. Many of these people had frightening experiences with wildlife as my mother found out back in the '30s while picking cranberries on a swamp. As she picked, she felt a presence and turned to find a cougar crouched about 20 feet away, sneaking toward her. Terrified, she did the only thing she could think of and started banging her berry pails together as hard as she could. It took a few minutes, but the beast finally moved away and let her return home, thoroughly shaken.

Some woodsmen had strange experiences. Prince George trapper Harry Weaver, for example, who noticed a moose continually hanging around the same swamp in 1936. Unable to get an adequate

Bessie Boudreau with cougar. c.1940.

amount of food, this animal was starving to death. Harry finally went for a closer look and found that the front hooves of the moose had grown well out from its feet and then curled up about ten inches. The poor beast was unable to walk in the forest. Pictures of these moose feet are included in this book.

One problem I ran into was trying to avoid confusion with the names of streams, because so many have been changed throughout the years. For instance, what was the Big Salmon River is now the McGregor. The Bear River and Bear Lake have been changed to Bowron, and so on.

Some of the terminology used in this book may be hard to understand by people who are not familiar with life in the wilds, so I will try to explain some terms and expressions.

The terms main cabin and line cabin are used frequently. A main cabin applies to the principal residence in their guiding or trapping area, while a line cabin refers to a small, often remote cabin that may have been visited only occasionally. Some trappers and guides only had one cabin. Ole Hansen, on the other hand, had 27. Some camped under a lean-to or in the open wherever night caught them. Others went to great length to make their camps as cozy and homey as possible.

Another term that may need explaining is 'rubbed.' When referring to fur, it means that a patch of fur is missing or very thin, rendering it of little or no commercial value. A foot-log is just a tree lying across a stream that has been stripped of its branches so it can be used to walk on. A bug is another term many will not be familiar with. It is a lighted candle placed inside a tin can with one end cut out so the light of the burning candle can shine out. The candle, as it burns away, is continually pushed up through a hole cut in the bottom of the can. Some woodsmen used two candles if they needed more light or heat, and they got a surprising amount of both from these. A strong gust of wind would blow the candles out, so matches or lighter had to be kept readily available. Other than that, they were absolutely foolproof.

The word 'sticky,' when applied to snowshoeing, means the kind of snow that sticks to the snowshoes and makes for a tiring day in the forest. The term 'billy can' refers to a pail that was hung over the fire to cook with or for making coffee or tea.

Most of the area I deal with lies east of Prince George, along the Fraser and McGregor Rivers. The Torpy River as well as the Slim Lake area are also frequently mentioned. This area comprises some of the toughest walking in the province, with Sitka alder thickets along the mountains that are so impenetrable they can make a grizzly bear swear. Below the alder swales, seas of Devil's Club await the hiker with a million barbs at their disposal. People can get frustrated to the point where they will kick angrily at them, only to find they are branched and that their twin strikes back viciously in return. Several species of flies, including horseflies, patrol steadily throughout the day. About sundown they go off shift, but the mosquitoes and little no-see-ums stay around to make life interesting. Aside from that, it is a world of wonder that I wouldn't trade for any place on earth.

Finally, if I were to point to any one thing as being the most difficult thing these people had to face, I think it would be loneliness: an insidious, continuous malady that can eat at a person's mind until madness or suicide ensues. Probably the biggest surprise I encountered in this work was the large number of so-called trapper suicides. So-called, I say, because in many suspected suicides, furs appeared to have gone missing.

Jack Boudreau

1

THE RIVER

FROM THE TIME OF THE CONSTRUCTION OF THE GRAND Trunk Pacific Railway until the completion of Highway 16, there were only two modes of transportation in the Penny/Dome Creek area: the railroad and the Fraser River. Throughout my youth it was not uncommon to hear the motors of river boats in the dead of night as they headed for whichever community happened to have a dance or party at that particular time. It was as natural as breathing that we became proficient with these river boats, and just as important was the ability to read the water. Use of the river and the railroad being so extensive, it seems that a bit of history of both is in order.

Aside from a few explorers, prospectors, and trappers, the Fort George area stayed silently remote from the rest of the world. The first hint of change occurred in 1871 when the sternwheeler *Enterprise* came through on its journey up the Nechako River in an attempt to service the Omineca gold fields. Although it failed that objective, it was a great navigational achievement in that it reached Takla Lake. It was finally abandoned on the shore of Trembleur Lake.

However the Blackwater Trail remained the lifeline of Fort George although the Indians sometimes brought scow loads of supplies upriver from Quesnel. These trips against the river current were almost impossible, and in some cases took up to 19 days.

When the steamer *Charlotte* blew its whistle at Fort George in 1908, it heralded the dawn of a new age. When the steamer *Nechako* followed in 1909, history was made. Not only did this gallant vessel brave the Nechako to Stoney Creek in June but in October, it went up the east fork of the Fraser and challenged the Grand Canyon, which had until that time been considered impassable. Captain Bonsor lined his craft through the canyon and continued on to the head of the Goat River Rapids 201 miles upstream of Fort George and had it not been

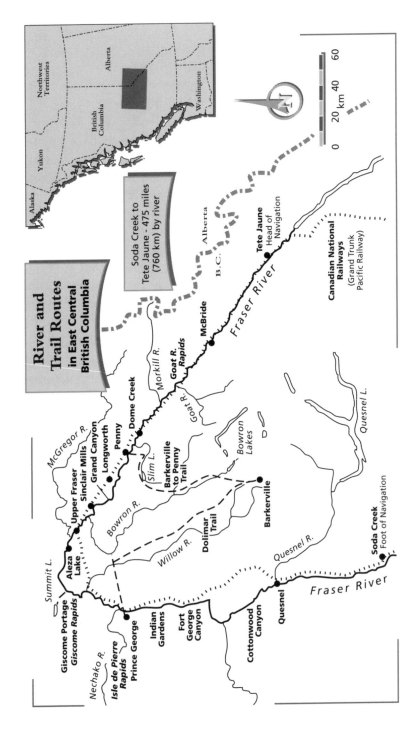

River and
Trail Routes
in East Central
British Columbia

Soda Creek to
Tete Jaune - 475 miles
(760 km) by river

Canadian National
Railways
(Grand Trunk
Pacific Railway)

Tete Jaune
Head of
Navigation

Fraser River

McBride

Alberta

B.C.

Northwest
Territories

Alberta

British
Columbia

Washington

Yukon

Alaska

20 km 40   60

0

Morkill R.

Goat R.
Rapids

Dome Creek

Penny

Longworth

Grand Canyon

Sinclair Mills

Upper Fraser

McGregor R.

Goat R.

Slim L.

Barkerville
to Penny
Trail

Bowron
Lakes

Quesnel L.

Bowron R.

Willow R.

Dolimar
Trail

Barkerville

Summit L.

Aleza
Lake

Giscome Portage
Giscome Rapids

Isle de Pierre
Rapids
Prince George

Nechako R.

Indian
Gardens

Fort
George
Canyon

Quesnel R.

Cottonwood
Canyon

Quesnel

Soda Creek
Foot of Navigation

Fraser River

for low water, he would have taken his load of freight right to Tête Jaune, the head of navigation on the Fraser River.

The year 1909 was also the beginning of the attempt to clear the river of obstructions to navigation when $20,000 was spent at Fort George Canyon. Only a few rocks were blown from the channel and a portage trail cut, leading many people to suggest that the money had been wasted.

Pressure on the stagecoach line from Quesnel was relieved in 1910 with the arrival of the palatial steamer the *BX*, which began service biweekly between Soda Creek and Fort George, the price of a ticket being $17.50. This opened a new chapter in transportation with passengers then able to make the trip from Vancouver to Fort George in under 35 hours: Vancouver to Ashcroft by train, Ashcroft to Soda Creek by auto, and Soda Creek to Fort George by steamer.

Margaret and Gus Lund at fishing heaven, Trembleur Lake, 1932.

The *BX* was joined on this run by the steamer *Chilcotin* which got off to a bad start while lining itself up through the Fort George Canyon: a young lad had placed the winch cable on a tree at river's edge and when the line was tightened, it pulled the tree over, killing the poor fellow. On its return trip downriver, the steamer struck a rock at this same canyon and had to be pulled from service for the rest of the year.

In May 1910 the steamer *Charlotte* had an even worse run of luck that began when its winch cable slipped off the pin on the Fort George Canyon wall. The ship swung around, struck a rock, and punched a good-sized hole in its side, allowing water to pour in. Repaired and back in service by June, it again struck a rock at the same canyon, this time with such force that the boiler shifted forward breaking the connections. This resulted in the entire vessel being enveloped in steam, causing a panic among the passengers. Captain Alexander coolly brought the steamer to the shore where it was quickly repaired once again.

Steamships BX and BC Express. The Express often travelled between Fort George and Tête Jaune Cache, lining through the Grand Canyon. After 1914 its route was from Fort George south to Soda Creek.

Two months later, the *Charlotte* was again in an accident in the same canyon: although no jar or bump was felt, she began filling with water and the captain was forced to beach her. After the basic repairs were made, an attempt was made to get her back to Quesnel. At one point it was necessary to tear out all the partitions on the lower deck just to get enough fuel to keep the pumps and the main engine going. After a thorough inspection in Quesnel, the proud old steamer yielded to the three-strikes-you're-out rule and went into a well-deserved retirement.

In October 1910, the *BX* hit a rock above the same canyon with the result that several bulkheads were bashed in. Only the watertight compartments present on the vessel kept it from being destroyed.

The year 1910 saw the small steamer *Fort Fraser* be the first to make the trip to Tête Jaune, a distance of 315 miles from Fort George. It was also the year when the boat explored the Nechako all the way to Fort Fraser.

It was also in late 1910 that the steamer *Nechako* (renamed *Chilko*) attempted to bring a shipment of freight from Quesnel only to find Fort George Canyon blocked with ice. The boat was beached six

Wreck of S.S. Charlotte, one mile below Fort George Canyon, July 1910.
BC Provincial Archives photo #58425.

miles upstream from the mouth of the Blackwater River where most of the freight was unloaded and taken ashore. Unfortunately ice jammed up at the mouth of the river which caused the water level to rise about 12 feet, breaking the *Chilko* free of its moorings. When last seen that fall, only the pilot house and woodwork could be seen above the water. In April a crew managed to refloat the damaged vessel and got it under steam only to have a boiler tube blow. Helpless, the steamer drifted into Cottonwood Canyon where it became lodged in the ice. The crew were able to get ashore on the ice, but the *Chilko* was ground to bits and disappeared from view. The 37,000 pounds of off-loaded freight had been hauled to Fort George during the winter.

The prime contractors for the Grand Trunk Pacific Railroad were Foley Bros., Welch and Stewart (FWS) and at this time they were moving great quantities of freight and supplies downriver from Tête Jaune to service their caches. These caches were well stocked to supply the needs of the many surveyors employed in laying out the grade. Scow operators were fortunate to make three trips a year, as it took two to three weeks to paddle or pole their way up to Tête Jaune where they built scows and then headed downriver to the various caches. The number of drownings at this stage caused the news media to scream for signs to be erected at the Giscome Rapids, the Grand Canyon, as well as the Goat River Rapids.

Running scows down the river was tough enough but in September, 1911, a scow owned by A. Bourchier left Fort George heading upstream for Tête Jaune Cache, 315 miles distant. Aboard were 16,000 pounds of merchandise for a general store which Mr. Bourchier planned to open there. The crew of four white men and three Indians made the trip in 32 days.

The effort made by the news media finally began to take effect, and in September 1911, Fred Hayden — employed by the Federal Department of Works — arrived at Fort George Canyon where he began work on the reef that partially blocked the eastern channel. This work lasted throughout the winter until February when three sunken shafts were cross-sectioned and blown using 36 cases of dynamite.

During the winter of 1911-12, FWS rebuilt two steamers at Tête Juane. Having finished their work on the Skeena River, the *S.S.*

Operator and the *S.S. Conveyor* steamed to Vancouver where they were dismantled and moved to Tête Jaune. About two hundred men were employed in this rebuilding operation and the costs were staggering. All the fir timbers had to be shipped from the coast via Edmonton and the boilers, which each weighed 50,000 pounds, had to be shipped from Vancouver and then hauled the last 20 miles: one with a donkey engine, and the other with twelve teams of horses. In one spot it took three days to move the boilers a distance of one mile. These steamers were 145 feet long with a beam of 47 feet, each motor produced 600 horsepower. Each vessel was capable of carrying 200 tons, as well as towing 150 tons on scows. With ease they handled 90 ton steam shovels on barges, towing them to wherever they were needed.

One more steamer was added to the fleet in 1912 when the BC Express Company, which held the Royal Mail contract, launched the *BC Express*. This boat was designed specifically for the upriver run between Fort George and Tête Jaune and was the most powerful of its size on the river. With a length of 140 feet and a beam of 28 feet, it was powered by a 265 horsepower engine. It had a passenger capacity of 150 and could carry an additional load of 110 tons of freight. Perhaps its best asset was its 16 inch empty draught which made it ideal for the Tête Jaune run. It was the first vessel to carry a load of freight to Tête Jaune, and the only one to deliver a scheduled service between there and Fort George.

During the summer of 1912 a powder expert, Frank Freeman, started downriver from Tête Jaune with a crew of men. Their task was to clear the river of log-jams and boulders which threatened the scows and steamers. They were clearing a channel in the Grand Canyon when the *Operator,* loaded with 150 tons of freight, smashed on a rock in the Goat River Rapids. The crew had to jettison over 100 tons of freight just to save the vessel from total destruction. Frank's crew was moved back to the rapids where they blasted out a clear channel for the boats.

After he finished work at the Goat River Rapids, Frank returned to the Grand Canyon and continued his blasting program which had a surprising effect. After a couple sets of small falls about two feet high in the upper canyon were blown away by the powdermen, it then became apparent that the water flow had increased in speed by three or four miles per hour. While this helped the steamers somewhat, it did nothing for the scows and rafts, nor for the dugout canoes.

Completing his work at the canyon, Frank moved his crew up the Nechako River where he tackled the Mud and Isle de Pierre Rapids. By November, with a crew of 14 men, he was trying to clear a channel through the Giscome Rapids — an awesome undertaking when it is realized that these rapids stretch along the Fraser for a distance of seven miles. At this same time, another 10 men under W. McLaren were blasting and clearing boulders from Indian Gardens, six miles down the Fraser from Fort George.

The character and fortitude of the people travelling the waterways at that time was summed up quite nicely by Prince George pioneer Ted Williams, whose father George Williams was among the best of the river pilots during construction of the Grand Trunk Pacific, and had passed on this story which Ted related to me: "A man named John Fountain who had timber holdings in the Clearwater area was with my father when they had a funny experience in 1911. They were coming down the Fraser by canoe from Tête Jaune Cache when they caught up with an Irishman who had left the Cache over one day ahead of them. As they came around a bend in the river they were surprised to hear someone singing. They looked over and here was this guy sitting in the crutch of a partly submerged tree near the shore singing songs about Ireland. This guy's raft had come apart when it hit the submerged tree and he was stuck up in that tree all night and didn't seem the least bit worried." Ted laughed and then concluded, "This fellow didn't know they were coming down the river. He could have been there for days. And another thing, he was so cold that they had to take him ashore, make a fire and warm him up before they could continue downriver, yet there he was sitting up there singing."

This man was very lucky compared to many others whose rafts came apart. Drownings were a common occurrence in 1911 and 1912. But the worst was yet to come, for in one week from late May to early June 1913, there were seven reported drownings: two near

Willow River and five at the Grand Canyon. Newspapers screamed that unless the government did some immediate protection work, hundreds would perish before ice again jammed the river.

The amount of traffic on the river at that time was quite surprising. Newspaper articles state that rafts were arriving in Fort George every day; the new arrivals were often quite surprised to find that the best pieces of land were already taken.

But along the river, rafts, scows, and canoes were breaking up and the bodies of the drowned were often never recovered. This led one of the more experienced rivermen to say, "The rapids do not give up their dead."

Of all the rough water in the rapids and canyons, the Grand Canyon was by far the most treacherous piece of water with Green's Rock in the upper canyon frequently tearing scows and rafts to pieces. Down below waited the giant whirlpool which at certain water levels stretched clear across the river. The channels that had been blasted out at great expense were of little or no value to inexperienced scow men, boat, or raft operators who didn't know where the channels were and could not see them in the dirty river water.

The August 2, 1913 edition of the *Fort George Herald* contained the following story:

"George Williams, the wizard of the Fraser River arrived in town again this week from the end of steel bringing down another large consignment of merchandise for Kennedy, Blair and Co. a local mercantile dealer. G. Williams, together with William McLaren, and Bob Alexander, both well known rivermen, have brought down over 60 scows from the head since the opening of navigation this spring and have not lost a pound of freight. Over 1000 tons of freight have been landed here by these men and their crews. Asked the question of the number of scows that have come downriver since navigation opened, Mr. Williams placed the total at about 1000. These scows cost about $250, contain about 2,000 feet of lumber, and carry about 25 tons of freight.

"A tremendous amount of freight has been lost along the river through the operations of inexperienced scow men. The Bates Rogers Construction Company has lost hundreds of tons of cement for their bridge work, and FW and Stewart (FWS) are reported to have lost enough material to pay for the construction of two large steam boats. The river is now at a good stage for scowing, said Mr. Williams, and he expects to land another thousand tons of freight for his employers before the end of the season."

In fairness to the other scow men, it must be noted that Mr. Williams and Mr. Alexander had gasoline-powered launches which were part of the 14 such launches on the upper portion of the river. The two big steamers — *Operator* and *Conveyor* moved the scows downriver to the FWS cache at the head of the Grand Canyon where the freight was hauled around the upper canyon on a tramway; then moved downriver with the launches. This virtually eliminated the loss of lives and supplies for these men, but for those not blessed with motorized launches, it was a much different story.

In a speech to his fellow Rotarians in 1951, this same George Williams, now a Prince George merchant, told how long ropes were used to guide the scows into safe channels. Part of his speech follows: "...Experienced crewmen would often return overland after shooting the canyon and guide transient scows through the boiling rock-strewn

Left to right: S.S. Chilcotin and S.S. Conveyor at Foley Bros., Welch & Stewart Dock at Island Cache, Prince George, 1913.

BC Provincial Archives photo

river. Fees for this service ranged from $300 to $500 and resulted in bitter rivalry between FW and Stewart pilots and the independents.

"Often two scows would be lashed together to keep them from capsizing in swift water. Even this precaution did not entirely eliminate the danger, and on at least one occasion one of the boats was swamped and threatened to pull the other craft under. A quick-witted river hog [pilot] slashed at the bindings with an axe and allowed the other craft to float free.

"Stranded crewmen, their boats swamped or smashed, would often continue downriver with the aid of a flimsy raft of logs held together by ropes or baling wire. But not all of them were that fortunate: rock or canyon walls were dotted with the hulls of crumpled scows, mute testimony to the fate of their crews. In the first summer's operation, I had first-hand knowledge of 17 rivermen who perished in the raging water after their boats had been lost. Certainly many more met a similar fate..."

The pilots referred to by Mr. Williams are no doubt the independents under Joe McNeil, the man who originally organized them. Called Canyon Cats, some of these pilots made a great deal of money at their trade. Fred Bennett, George Booth, and Norman Rooney were some. Mr. Rooney claimed he earned over $3000 in three months in 1913. When compared to labourers on the grade at $2.00 per day and skilled workmen at up to $5.00, these Canyon Cats were truly an elite group.

Many people coming downriver were suspicious that there was in fact no rough water, and that these pilots were nothing more than scoundrels trying to separate them from their meagre savings. Once they had made this decision they would carry on, oblivious to the warnings of others, and only when they found the vertical canyon walls rising up around them did they — in terror — realize the enormity of their error.

Early in 1913, a provincial constable was stationed at the head of the Grand Canyon. He refused to let small boats or rafts go through unless they were portaged or lined down through the worst water. Scow loads were restricted to a maximum of 15 tons, and four-by-eight foot signs were finally placed above the canyon, as well as above the Goat River and Giscome Rapids. These signs warned of the dangers below, as well as the safe channels to be taken. Even with all these precautions, the death rates continued and already in June, the 1913 death rate stood at over 20 in the Grand Canyon alone.

Although several sternwheelers tried to climb the upper canyon, the SS Conveyor was the only one to succeed. On four different occasions it climbed the upper canyon under its own power in less than 15 minutes. When the SS Hammond attempted the feat, it found itself at a standstill right in the fastest water. Only by getting a line to shore was disaster averted.

A story with a rather odd twist began unfolding at the canyon in 1913 when two Frenchmen, Maurice Streiff and Samuel Tonduz, were reported drowned in the Grand Canyon. Following the publication of the article in many newspapers, the Belgian Consulate in Edmonton was requested to investigate, and so Maurice Poldt was sent out to recover the bodies if possible. After arriving in Fort George on the steamer BC Express from Tête Jaune, Mr. Poldt began searching the bunkhouses and lunch counters along the river front, hoping to find some word about the missing men. Suddenly, he walked right into Mr. Tonduz, who informed him that they had indeed lost their scow in the canyon but had both managed to escape. Mr. Streiff, a man of considerable import in France, was somewhere along the river heading for Tête Jaune and eventually Edmonton. Mr. Poldt was then informed that it was only by a weird stroke of fate that Mr. Tonduz was in town. It seems that after escaping the river he had taken a job working on the grade, and one day while he was watching a blast, a piece of rock flew and pierced the heart of an Italian standing right beside him. He had quickly decided that was not the place for him and had walked to town.

It wasn't all doom and gloom along the river, though, as some homesteaders found out in June 1913 when they found a fully loaded scow floating by with no one aboard. They towed the derelict ashore and began unloading a wealth of supplies. Their fun was eventually interrupted, however, when another scow appeared carrying the original scow men. It seems the sweeps, or large oars, had been torn out of their hands by the mighty current and they had transferred to an adjacent scow right in the heart of the canyon. The homesteaders only gave up their prize with great reluctance, feeling that it should be a matter of finders/keepers.

By July 1913 after many more deaths attributed to inexperienced scow men, all scows had to have two experienced pilots before they were allowed to run the canyon.

One of the canyon pilots, A. H. Dieber, better known as Sandbar Slim, had a narrow escape while running the upper canyon: he had one of the sweeps break and his scow slammed into Green's Rock with such force that the deck was torn off and thrown into the worst part of the current with him on it. Only by the greatest luck did the two pieces come back together again and Slim was able to get back aboard and make it to safety.

Along the grade adjacent to the river, the four hospitals set up for the railway workmen were often full to overflowing. With disease in the camps and injuries, the medical staff were kept busy. The many graves along the right-of-way and in the hospital cemeteries attest to the fact that they often fought a losing battle.

Although a great many blasts were set off in the river to remove obstacles, by far the biggest blast was set off about 24 miles east of Fort George along the railway grade. At a spot called Point of Rock, which had been an original FWS cache, a rock cliff stretched down to the water's edge. In September 1913, 200 tons of dynamite were exploded there and when the dust settled, there was the new grade. So precise was the blast that the Cache, only 100 yards distant, remained untouched by flying rock.

In the construction camps along the right-of-way, the police often had their hands full. There were always those who tried to separate the workers from their pay. In June 1913 John Hooper was arrested and charged with having liquor for sale in a construction camp. The May 3, 1913 edition of the *Fort George Herald* quoted the judge as saying: "I don't think that any man travelling around among railway gangs with 90 bottles of whiskey in his trunks can expect anyone to presume that he had it for his own needs, ...I think it is a serious matter for a man to have two suitcases full of whiskey in a construction camp. It leads to murder in the wilds and all kinds of trouble. You should live there for a while, as I have done, to find out what it means. If I am wrong, the court of appeals can set me right." Mr. Hooper was given a choice of a $300 fine or 12 months in jail. He paid the fine.

For the steamers, 1913 was to be their last year working above Fort George. Contrary to navigation regulations, the railroad put in two low-level bridges, one at Dome Creek and the other at Hansard. This eliminated any chance of competition. The BC Express Company fought the railroad in the courts for several years but it appears it was a done deal. Eventually in November 1918, their damage claim of $7500 was denied. Barred from upriver work, their two steamers— BX and BC Express—along with the two big steamers— Operator and Conveyor, worked the river between Prince George and Soda Creek, servicing the construction camps of the Pacific Great Eastern Railway as well as Quesnel and Soda Creek, 160 miles downriver. As for the upper portion of the mighty Fraser, the great sternwheelers faded away into one of the most romantic chapters in our history.

As is often the story, the steamer companies were not the only ones hurt by the closure of river traffic: in many places along the river, houses were constructed, cafes or rooming houses built in anticipation of continuous river traffic. The great number of deserted homesteads that lie in ruin along the waterway testify to the broken dreams that are often the price paid for monopoly.

Ray Mueller in Grand Canyon on Fraser River, 1953.

Perhaps in memory of these gallant vessels we can sit some quiet evening on the bank of this great river and watch them as they file past: *The Enterprise; Charlotte; Nechako (Chilco); BC Express; BX; Chilcotin; Quesnel (The Doctor); Fort Fraser; Operator; Conveyor;* and *Hammond.* Watch them steam away into the river mists of time.

Down through the years since railway construction, there have been a great many rivermen who have read the water. But for me, there is one man who stands out as the one who deserves the right to be called Mr. Canyon: Ray Mueller. Ray and his wife Louisa moved to Sinclair Mills in 1944 and settled on the bank of what was originally called the Tonaquah River, later renamed Moxley Creek after the turn-of-the-century trapper and timber baron Karl Moxley. Located only about 10 miles below the Grand Canyon, Ray spent much of the next 45 years travelling these rough waters as a guide, trapper, and also as a riverman who moved log drives along the river for the logging companies.

It would seem that after all those years of teasing the water-gods that this would be where his greatest personal danger lay, but that was not the case: his closest brush with disaster happened when he was going out on his trapline on an wheeled Bombardier machine, one of the forerunners of the modern snowmobile. In order to cross a stream, Ray had to climb the Canadian National Railway grade. Just after he had passed the stream, the machine tipped over and rolled to the bottom of the grade, pinning him beneath it. As most of the weight was resting on his chest, he found it extremely difficult to breathe. With all his strength he tried to roll the machine, but to no avail. The movement did help to change his position in the snow, however, making it easier to breathe. For several hours he alternately fought and rested, knowing he could not survive overnight in the cold. During his attempts, the section crew had passed by right above him but they had not noticed him or the machine. He kept moving and fighting until he finally managed to free one arm, just as the section crew returned from their patrol. He frantically waved his free arm and by the greatest bit of luck, one of the men saw it and they rushed to his rescue.

In 1966, Ray blasted the top off of the infamous Green's Rock in the Grand Canyon because it was continually causing logjams right in the worst part of the canyon. Just why the powdermen didn't blow it during construction is a mystery. It seems that many lives could have been saved and much property loss could have been avoided.

It was also in 1966 that I spent some time working with Ray and his son Don, driving logs along the river. One day after we had broken a logjam right in the canyon, I said to Ray: "A lot of people must have drowned here during railway construction."

"They sure did," he responded with his usual dry sense of humour. "As a matter of fact, on a clear day you can still see four or five bodies going around in the eddy."

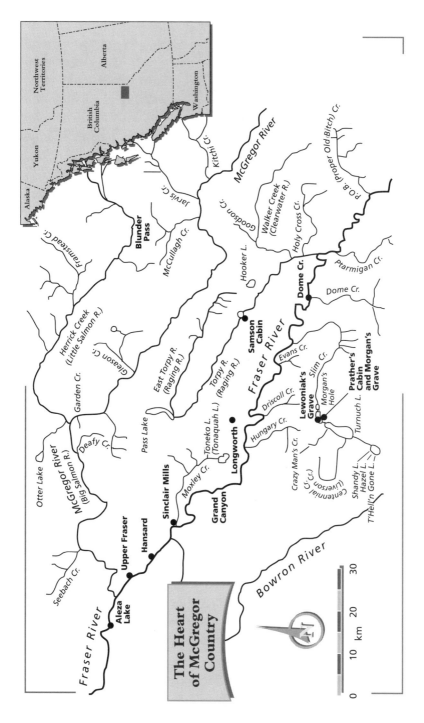

The Heart of McGregor Country

2

THE MᶜGREGOR

THE INFLUX OF PEOPLE INTO THE INTERIOR OF BC, whether they came by railroad, stagecoach, sternwheeler, raft or canoe was comprised of many adventurous souls. One of the men who arrived seemed to be born for a life of adventure. His name was Ole Anund Hansen.

Born in Horten, Norway, Ole became restless at a very young age. As several family members were merchant marines, Ole took it upon himself to steal aboard a vessel that was captained by his uncle. Just a short distance out to sea he was discovered and returned to his family. The attempt to keep him at home failed, though, and a year later it was his mother who packed his belongings and bid him goodbye. At the tender age of 14 he walked away from the homeland, he would not see again for another 60 years.

Aboard a ship where he was training to be a steam engineer, Ole sailed on several seas and then the Atlantic Ocean, eventually ending up in Boston. While there he noticed posters of western Canada, the advertisements stating that it was a land of opportunity. Through immigration he got an opportunity to come to Canada on the promise that he would work on a farm in Saskatchewan for one year. When that year was up, Ole knew two things for certain: he was not going to be a farmer, and he was going to head west. He travelled to Vancouver and then came north, arriving in Fort George on the BC Express stagecoach in 1909.

The first couple of years after he arrived were spent doing a variety of different jobs: he freighted with dog teams and horses in winter and worked with scows along the river in summer. Much of this time he worked with Billy Seymour, husband of Granny Seymour of South Fort George, famous for her longevity.

In 1911 he moved his family to Hansard, BC. In 1912 he began trapping the Big Salmon (now McGregor) River 68 miles up the

Fraser from Fort George. His trapping, and later his guiding line, stretched from the mouth of the river to the first canyon about 25 miles upriver. The following year he guided his first hunting party into this same area which contained some of the best game country imaginable. Thus began a life adventure of trapping and guiding that was to cover the next 52 years of his life.

Ole's first five years in the McGregor were spent without cabins, camping wherever night found him and his hunters. This changed as he eventually built and maintained 27 cabins, a clear indication of the incredibly active life he led.

Of all the stories that Ole told me, I think my favorite was the story of Society Red. It happened during the winter of 1915-16 when a stranger came up the McGregor River and began trapping the area of Otter Creek and…well, here's Ole:

> "This man never offered his name, but being that he had red hair and always talked about how he had travelled in high society back in the States, well, he earned the handle of Society Red. He brought along a huge dog that weighed about 150 pounds, a true friend that would prove to be worth more than its weight in gold.

From left to right: unknown, Bill Yost, Caribou John, Martin Framstead, Mr. Duncan and Ole Hansen at Martin Framstead's cabin, two miles above James Creek.

"Red built a cabin at the confluence of Otter Creek and the McGregor River, and then began trapping. In January he was in the area of Otter Lake when he took a terrible fall and fractured a leg. He was several miles from his cabin with just a limited amount of food, and he knew that he was in deep trouble. After getting over the initial shock, he fashioned some splints, set his leg, and then tied it up with strips of canvas he cut out of his pack.

"Just as it was getting dark that same evening," Ole continued, "a moose walked right up to him like it had been sent from heaven and saved his life. He shot the moose and cut off part of the hide which he used to make a shelter. Then, with food and shelter, he started to believe that he had a chance. For six weeks he stayed put in the shelter, with the dog providing more than enough heat to keep him warm. During this time he built a toboggan out of the moose hide and a harness for the dog. Well, he stayed in that shelter for six weeks, and when he felt good enough to travel, that powerful dog pulled him all the way back to his cabin on the river.

"That spring when several of us trappers got together we realized that no one had seen Red for several months, and we naturally assumed that some bad fortune had befallen him. As soon as the ice went off the river, another trapper named Blackie Lawrence and I poled a boat up the river to Red's cabin and found him there in good spirits. Man! Was he overjoyed to see us. He went into great detail about his winter ordeal, and I couldn't help but notice the constant attention that he lavished on his dog. I felt that he put it quite well when he said, "He didn't just save my life, he kept me warm and kept me company, too.

"We took Red out to medical attention in Prince George," Ole added, "but it was unnecessary, as the doctor found that he had done an excellent job of splinting the fracture himself.

"Also, this Blackie Lawrence fellow left the McGregor area the following year and moved to the Northwest Territories where, just a few years later, he was killed in his sleeping bag by his own dog team."

As I was most interested in grizzly bears, I asked Ole about their numbers in the early years. "Well, for the first quite a few years we had to climb up near timberline to get grizzlies. In fact, I think it was up until 1930, but afterwards we could get all we wanted right down along the valley bottom. I feel that the reason for this, in part, must have been something to do with the decline of the caribou and the massive increase in the moose populations which live at lower altitudes. This may have had something to do with bringing the grizzlies down."

One of Ole's favorite memories took him back to the year 1920. "I had an American hunter with me at the time, and I was trying to find a grizzly bear for him. We were camped right up at the timberline, and as we sat there by the campfire talking, a large pack of wolves began howling in the timber a short distance below us. After several minutes they quieted down and then the hunter turned to me and said, 'Just sitting here by the campfire listening to those wolves howling has been a complete wilderness adventure all by itself'."

The following story was told to me by Ole's daughter, Ruth. I don't know if Ole forgot to tell me this one or if he just deliberately wanted to forget it. "It was during the winter of 1930 that Dad got into a situation that almost cost him his life: it started when he got a horrible axe cut on his leg while splitting firewood, and it got much worse when he sewed the cut together with black thread. Infection set in, and in desperation, he set out on snowshoes for his nearest neighbour, John Bergstrom. Stumbling and dragging himself along, he arrived at John's cabin right at the point of collapse. The infection had turned to septicemia, which in turn prompted John to take drastic action. Assuming that the dye in the black thread may be the main cause of the problem, and since he had nothing else to work with but black thread, he boiled the thread. Then, using a heated knife to sear the flesh and prevent bleeding, he went to work. He removed the stitches, cut away the infected flesh as carefully as possible, and sewed up the wound with the boiled thread. With Dad passing in and out of delirium, John used combinations of hot compresses and raw meat applied directly to the wound. Over a period of several weeks, John cared for and nursed Dad back to health until he had completely recovered. Years later, Dad picked no bones about the fact that John had saved his life."

I asked Ole about the sizes of the biggest grizzlies he had seen, and he came back with this story. "It was mid-October, 1947 when this story took place. We were at my main cabin at Seabach Creek, and I had two hunters from Spokane, Washington with me. One of these men had previously been guided by me and had brought a friend along to share his good fortune, as he had done quite well on the previous hunt. By the end of the second day, this original hunter had already taken his moose and bear, so on the third day, he decided to fish Seabach Creek while I took his friend up river to try for a moose."

Really into this story, Ole went on. "Just a few miles along the river was an island with a three-acre meadow that was an excellent spot for moose, and it was here that we came upon a big bull. The hunter shot the moose and we proceeded to dress it out. When we finished, I put the heavy moose antlers on my pack board and carried them back out to the riverboat. At this time, we built a campfire, made tea, and ate lunch. All this time, a light breeze carried the smoke from our campfire all over the small island, and I would have thought that there wouldn't be an animal within miles." Ole said.

"After we had finished eating lunch, we returned to the quartered moose with the pack board with which I was going to pack out the meat. I left my 30-06 rifle at the riverboat, but the hunter brought his .32 special along. After tying a quarter of moose meat on the pack board, I got the hunter to give a lift to get the pack on my back. No sooner had we lifted the pack onto my back, then we heard a mighty roar and saw a huge grizzly come charging out of the alders straight at us. I glanced at the hunter whose face had gone chalk white, and yelled, 'Climb a tree!' Then I slipped out of the pack board, letting it fall to the ground. The bear immediately attacked the pack, delivering a few vicious blows, then with one powerful slap, it sent the quarter of meat sailing through the air. No sooner had it hit the ground, then the bear jumped on it again and administered a few more slaps. As it was very wet on the island, I had been wearing hip-waders which made for very difficult climbing. But I'm telling you that I went right up a pine tree about 20 feet above the ground."

Realizing that he had my undivided attention, he carried on. "When the grizzly left the quarter of moose, its attention was immediately drawn to the hunter who was about 10 feet up in a thick spruce tree. He was making a hell of a racket, breaking limbs and screaming at the bear to go away. Somehow, he managed to take his rifle up the tree with him. When the bear stood up right beside him and let out a blood-curdling roar, he yelled out in a voice that sounded more like a woman than a man, 'Get away from me you son of a bitch!'

"Somehow, he got his rifle into position and fired all his bullets right into the bear's abdomen at point blank range. I could tell the bear was badly wounded, and after a few more loud roars, it turned and ran back into the alders and then everything was really quiet," Ole continued. "After waiting for several minutes, I told the hunter to stay put in the tree while I went back to the boat for my 30-06 but he wouldn't have any part of it. Instead, he shouted, 'No! Don't go. Please don't go. What if something happens to you? I'll die out here in this godforsaken woods!'

"After a 20-minute wait with no sound from the bear, I couldn't hang on any longer. I knew that if I didn't go down, that I was going to fall down, and I didn't want that. That hunter had fired all the bullets he had brought along, so he was no help. I slid down the tree, ran to the boat, came back with my rifle, then told the hunter to come down out of the tree, and when he was down, I told him to stay quiet while I tried to follow the bear. Again he refused and yelled, 'I don't want any goddamned bear, I just want to get the hell out of here, let's go home!' I took him back to the boat, untied the rope, told him to push off, and drift back to the cabin if anything went wrong. Then I went back and packed out all the moose meat. Finally at the insistence of the hunter, we returned to the cabin where he went into great detail telling his partner all about the day's adventure."

I was so into this story, that I think my mouth must have been hanging open, Ole was well aware of it as he went on. "The following morning, all three of us returned to the meadow where I followed the blood trail through the thick undergrowth. Not more than 60 feet from where it had been shot, I found the bear lying with its back up against a tree. I threw a few limbs at it to make certain it was dead, then walked over to it and found that it had just died, as it was still loose and warm. After calling the other men to come into the thicket, I proceeded to skin the bear. Then I said, 'By gosh! I've sure got myself a nice bear this time.' Well! You should have heard that hunter holler, 'What the hell do you mean? That's my bear. I shot that bear.'

"'Yes, you shot it,' I joked, 'but I definitely heard you say that you didn't want any damned bear.' That fellow was overjoyed when he saw the enormous size of that hide."

I asked Ole if he had measured the hide, and he said, "This was by far the biggest bear I ever laid eyes on. I guessed its weight at 1000 pounds. The pad width of the front paw was nine inches and the hide squared out at exactly nine feet, lying loose on the ground. As for that hunter, well, I never saw or heard from him again, and with an experience like that on his first hunt, I sure don't blame him."

Ole added an interesting footnote to this story. About two weeks earlier his son Anund had visited the same island with a hunter, and they had bagged a moose. A few days later they had returned and bagged a grizzly. This big grizzly had then moved in, cleaned up both the moose and grizzly carcasses and was looking for more when Ole and his hunter came along.

Ole also added that about five years later he saw another grizzly track with a nine-inch pad but as far as he knew, no one ever got it.

A good rule of thumb measurement for Interior adult boar grizzlies is a hide that squares just under eight feet and a weight of about 500 pounds for a spring bear and 600 pounds for a late fall bear. The square is obtained by measuring the hide in an opened position — the span across the front, claw to claw and the length from nose to tail. These two measurements are then added together and divided by two for the square. As for the front paw or pad width, an Interior adult boar will be about seven inches. The hind foot length, just under twelve. Anything over that is above average.

Another memory that brought a smile to Ole's face was the recollection of the time that a grizzly went into his riverboat and drank three gallons of outboard motor oil. A few days later it returned and tore the bottom off his canoe to get at the tar, which it ate.

Between Ole and his son Anund they took a total of 87 satisfied grizzly hunters through their guiding area. In one fall alone Anund took out 11 grizzly hunters and all connected.

Throughout the 52 years that he guided and trapped that area, Ole kept track of the moose he found that he felt were definitely killed by grizzly bears. The total was 82 or just under two per year.

In answer to my question about seeing unusual things, Ole responded: "Perhaps the most unusual thing that I ever saw in all my woods' experiences was a pack of about 30 wolves feeding on a moose on the ice of the river. As I watched, a large boar grizzly emerged from the forest and walked right up to the kill and started eating. Not only did he take the moose away, but he made the wolves suffer the ultimate indignity as well: he didn't even acknowledge their presence. They milled around and snarled at him as he began eating, and then them wolves, who enjoy putting fear in their victims, seemed puzzled. After putting up a bit of a show, they moved away into the forest."

"Were the boar grizzlies out most of the winter?" I asked.

"They were out at least ten months, depending on the weather. I think the main reason the boar grizzlies were out that much was because of the abundance of moose which they either took away from the wolf packs or killed for themselves. We never noticed any mothers and cubs around, though."

In early winter 1944, Ole experienced the most eventful day of his life. "I was walking along my trapline trail early one morning when I heard a long moaning sound in the forest ahead. It was the most mournful sound that I have heard in all my life. Several times it was repeated and although I didn't know what it was, I suspected it was a moose. I continued along my trail and entered an alder thicket that surrounded the trail for a quarter mile. About half way through the alder thicket I came to a spot where three trees lay criss-crossed on the trail. As I stepped over the trees, I spotted a grizzly 60 feet ahead, feeding on a moose it had killed. The grizzly spotted me at the same time, stood upright and let out a mighty roar. It was holding a freshly separated quarter of moose in its front paws. I tried to get the rifle off my pack board but the strap got caught in the teeth of a rolled up crosscut saw that I carried there. When I realized that I couldn't free the rifle, I just fired a shot into the air. This caused the grizzly to drop the moose meat it was holding and run into the forest."

Ole continued, "After I got settled down a bit, I started putting my pack board back on and then I heard something running toward me through the bush. I thought that it was the grizzly returning so I stood motionless with my rifle ready, and I was really shocked to see a moose come running straight at me, pursued by another grizzly. This was the answer to the moaning sound that I had heard earlier. This moose was in terrible condition with a large portion of a shoulder hanging down and flopping as it ran. The moose circled and stopped right behind me and I fired the rifle so that the bear wouldn't run right into me. When I shot, that bear jumped sideways and vanished into the thick alder undergrowth in a second: then I finished off the moose which would have died a slow death anyway.

"Well, I was convinced that I had experienced enough excitement for one day, so I put on my pack board and continued on toward the next cabin a few miles away." Ole continued. "When I got within one-half mile of the cabin, I saw fresh grizzly sign on the trail. I moved along carefully with my gun at the ready and came upon a man's rubber boot lying on the trail. Now that was just too damned much for one day. I was really shook up, I thought that the grizzly had just killed someone, and I hurried on to the cabin not sure what to do. Well, when I got to the cabin, I found that the bear had broken in there and the place was a terrible mess. I started cleaning the place up and that was when I found the other rubber boot. Then I remembered that it was one of a pair that had been left by a young Finlander who had trapped with me the previous winter. I realized then that it was the mate to the boot on the trail and that the grizzly had carried it there. After that, I was finally able to settle down a bit."

"That sure must have been a day to remember, a person wouldn't want very many like that," I suggested.

"No! That's for sure, and you know, later that day I found that the grizzly had been feeding on a moose it had killed only 100 yards from my cabin. Well, I can tell you for sure, that was the most exciting day of my life."

"Any other experiences with bears?" I asked.

"Lots. I recall the time I was checking my traps — this was in late November, it was the last trap to check before we got to one of my line cabins. I had a Finlander with me that I was teaching to trap and we both got a surprise that day. The trap was set in a hollow balsam tree and when I got close to it, I saw what I thought was a small wolverine. I pulled it out and gave it a tap on the head with the axe handle, then took a closer look and felt shivers run up and down my spine as I realized that I had caught a grizzly cub only three or four months old. I turned around in a few circles there, because I figured that the mother might be close by, and then I hurried to the cabin as I sure didn't want to tangle with her. Well that night several inches of snow fell and in the morning we carried on along the line. In the second trap that we checked, there was another grizzly cub about the same size, and the mother's fresh tracks could be seen heading up over the mountain. She didn't have any more cubs so I guess she just gave up and left."

"You're suggesting that these cubs were born in July?" I asked.

"Had to be about then. I don't know how that happened, but I don't think that mother would have lived out the winter if she had to feed those big cubs. I'm sure she would have died."

"I've found bear dens in the woods, lots of them in hollow cedar trees where black bears prefer to have their young. I've also found a freshly dug grizzly den in the mountains in September. Surely you must have found dens in all your years in the bush?" I asked.

"Several times." Ole went on. "The one that interested me the most was a grizzly den that was only 100 feet above the river. When I first found this den about 1913, it only went back into the bank about 10 or 12 feet. Over the next 50 years, several different grizzlies used it and each changed it to their own liking. When I last visited the den I found it penetrated the hill for a distance of about 20 feet. I also noticed that a lot of vegetation and coniferous boughs had been carried in."

"Was it easy to get game for your hunters, years ago?" I asked.

"We had very successful hunts. In 1951 for instance, we took out a Spanish diplomat and his wife, the American ambassador to Chile with his wife and their two sons, and of the four hunters, all got their moose, elk, caribou, and grizzly."

"Did you have any other scares out there besides confrontations with bears?" I asked.

"A person always has lots of scares, but one that comes to mind happened when I least expected it. I woke up one night when I heard a loud roaring noise and when I opened my eyes, I saw a bright light all around the cabin. It didn't take me very long to realize that the cabin was on fire. I jumped out of the bunk and went running out the door in my underwear, and there the roof of the cabin was on fire. Sparks from the stovepipe had caught the needles of a big spruce tree over the cabin, on fire. The burning needles fell and caught the cedar roofing on fire. While there was about a foot of snow on the ground, the big tree had kept the roof free of snow. I shoveled snow as fast as I could and finally managed to get the fire out, but not before I burnt a lot of holes in my underwear and almost froze to death. This was the only time I ever built a cabin under a tree, and you know that could have been the end of me. I didn't have time to put clothes on so if I hadn't got the fire out I'm sure I would have froze to death."

"Did you ever see any other confrontations between bears and wolves in your lifetime, Ole?"

"Well the bears and wolves often fed on the same carcasses at different times, but I know of a case where a big grizzly went and fed on a moose that the wolves had just killed and they didn't try to put up a fight, they just left. My son Anund had an American hunter with him one May when they saw where a mother grizzly with a baby cub had a bit of a battle with some wolves over a moose carcass. The sign was fresh in the snow and it looked like the bear got chased away by the wolves. Maybe she was afraid for her cub."

Ole offered much assistance to people building the Monkman Pass Highway and to surveyors working the Canadian Pacific Railway surveys through the area. He told me that the trappers and guides along the river were often called upon to help and feed very hungry travellers who emerged from the forest.

"You spent a lot of years running the rivers, Ole, did you ever have any close calls?"

"I almost drowned right at Upper Fraser back in the '50s. I had taken the Padlesky girls out for a ride with my riverboat and then dropped them off on shore. When I left them and headed downstream, I hit something — maybe a log under the water — and it flipped the boat right upside down. I managed to catch ahold of it and hang on but I had drunk a bit of water and was in trouble. Lucky for me, a riverman — I think his name was Kinishy — saw what happened and came out with the company riverboat and helped me out. You know if the girls had still been in the boat I think someone would have drowned.

"I was there when Harry Jackson drowned on the McGregor in the '30s." Ole went on. "That was a strange thing. He lived in Aleza Lake and was a real experienced boat operator. We had three boats and were freighting supplies for the Canadian Pacific Railway surveys through the Monkman Pass. We were just a short ways below Moose Creek and I was in the lead with Blackburn and Jackson following in their boats. We stopped and waited for them but they didn't show up, so we went back and found both boats at the bank. Apparently, Jackson's engine quit and then the boat lurched and tipped upside down pitching both men into the river. The fellow who was with him managed to hang onto the boat until it came to shore. Jackson started swimming, then hollered for help and went under, just like that. It wasn't even bad water where that happened. I don't know, that was a strange one."

Ole never seemed to have trouble remembering events through the years, so when I asked him if he had any other trouble with bears breaking into his cabins, he responded by telling me a story of a neighbouring trapper named Henry Hobi.

"It was in the fall of 1950, I think, when Henry Hobi took his winter supply of food up to his main cabin at Fontiniko Creek. He stored it in his boathouse, as he had done for many years and then he set out to prepare his line cabins for the winter's trapping season. This included stocking them with food, cutting firewood, and cutting trail wherever necessary. Two weeks later, he came back to find the boathouse had been broken into and all the food was gone. That same evening, he sat in wait and bagged a large black bear. Early the next morning, he bagged another black. Then he had to return all the way to Prince George to restock his winter grub supply. He figured that cost him about $600, and that was a lot of money back then."

After having several gab sessions with Ole, I paid a visit to Ego Bjorkland of Newlands, BC. He was on my wish list of people to talk to because he had spent several winters trapping with Ole during the Great Depression. Some of the stories he told me were duplicates of ones I'd already heard from Ole, but others were different, so I include them here.

"That first winter that I trapped with Ole, I was initiated into the life of a wilderness trapper in a hurry. It was in early December 1931, that we went hunting in an attempt to add some meat to our winter

Henry Hobi and Martin Framstead, expert axeman, both McGregor River trappers. c. 1935.

food supply. We went hunting and it wasn't very long before Ole had a caribou down. We dressed it out, and then each took a quarter of the animal on our pack boards and carried them back to the main cabin. We went back the next day for the rest of the meat, and walked right up to the carcass without noticing a grizzly bear that was lying down behind it. The bear had come at the carcass through the thick bush from the opposite direction so we had not seen its tracks in the snow, and we were completely caught off guard. All at once, the bear jumped up and let out a mighty roar, and it scared the hell out of us. We both managed to get a shot away and then the bear ran into the woods a bit and died. I tell you, my heart pounded that time. I sat down and had a rest. That was my introduction to the trapline."

Ego pointed out to me, as Ole had done previously, that the Seabach Creek area was absolutely loaded with bears in those days, both blacks and grizzlies, then he went on: "It was the next winter, in January 1932, that Ole and I left one of his line cabins and just a little while later we heard a pack of wolves howling in the distance. As we moved on along the line, we noticed that the pack of wolves kept getting closer and closer. Finally, they moved in all around us, howling continually. Several times we saw the entire pack when they crossed meadows or swamps, and we counted 35. Those wolves escorted us all the way to the main cabin, a distance of about three miles. As soon as we reached the cabin, we grabbed our rifles and ran back out, but the wolves had all vanished."

Ego summed it all up this way: "When that large pack of wolves surrounded us and started howling, I could feel it right down to my toes. I'm telling you that this was the only time in my life that I was really scared in the woods. That mournful howling all around us was very, very frightening."

In spite of this experience Ego stated that he was greatly impressed with wolves. He felt that they were extremely intelligent animals and though he agreed that they slaughtered a lot of game, he figured they were a necessary part of nature.

One of Ego's stories concerned a very interesting fellow that trapped the area of Otter Creek for many years. This gentleman's name was John Bergstrom. Ego's story begins:

"Just as many other trappers did, John used to go up in the ridges near his cabin and hunt caribou. On one hunt, he bagged one and then returned to his cabin for a pack board to carry it out with. Not one to rush into things, John sat down and thought about it for a while. Then he gathered up some cooking utensils and a few supplies, and headed back up the mountain to the caribou where he stayed until most of the meat had been consumed. From that time until his death at the age of 82, he was known to all the woodsmen as Caribou John."

"Yes. I've heard about him. In fact I remember travelling to Prince George on the trains years ago and seeing him standing by the tracks watching the train go by. I recall his nice bushy white beard." I said.

"That was him. I can tell you quite a few stories about him." Ego stated. "For instance, in February 1932 Ole and I decided to pay him a visit. We walked through the forest to where his cabin was, and it wasn't there. We looked around and saw some smoke coming out of a hole in the snow so we took a closer look. We found a tunnel going down into the snow to the door of the cabin so we started down making lots of noise so he wouldn't mistake us for an animal. He hadn't bothered to shovel out the cabin at all, you know. He just wasn't a very ambitious person. Well, he let us in and we couldn't see a thing in there because it was so dark. Ole suggested that a cup of coffee would sure hit the spot, but John said, 'I don't have any coffee but I've got lots of moose meat and flour, and besides, I've been making my own coffee out of dry leaves and that goes down not too bad.' Boy! You should have heard Ole change his mind in a hurry. We got out of there pretty quick after that."

"Did he even bother to trap at all?" I asked. "I mean trapping is pretty hard work."

"Oh, he trapped a bit all right, but that was fine because he had some good neighbours who helped out on his line from time to time." When Ego said that, I was almost certain that I detected a wink.

"Caribou was a real nice fellow, but I remember one year when he went to the store in Aleza Lake to get his winter grub supply, and the storekeeper cut him off. He hadn't been paying his grocery bill so the guy who owned the store — Lorne Lyle was his name —

would only let him charge flour and a few things. Well, Caribou went off to the trapline and came out the next spring with the best catch of his life, so that goes to show you."

After talking with Ego for a while, I asked him if anything funny happened on the line that he could remember and he told me this story with which I will close the adventures of Ole Hansen.

"It was in December 1932, when Ole walked out to Hansard to spend Christmas with his family and I stayed behind to run the trapline. On the day Ole was to return, I left on a trip around the line. A week later when I got back to the main cabin I found that he had not returned. I thought that something bad had happened to him along the trail so I set out toward home to search for him. I was snowshoeing along and all of a sudden I heard a strange sound in the woods. I listened for some time, but I couldn't make it out. I'd never heard anything like that in the woods before.

"Caribou"
John Bergstrom
at Otter Creek
main cabin,
c. 1935.

"It seemed to be coming in my direction so I just stood still and listened. Finally, I figured out what it was: it was Ole returning to the trapline, singing as loud as he could. I stood where I was and waited, and you know when Ole spotted me he didn't even stop, he just kept right on walking, and I could hear the sound of his voice echoing through the forest. There was no question about it, he had been into the Christmas cheer."

I was not surprised when Ego told me that Ole was not only a first class trapper, but also an excellent woodsman, and very easy to get along with. Coming from a fellow trapper who shared the cabins with him for years, I considered this an ultimate compliment.

I kept right after Ego about Caribou John, as I had already heard many stories about this most interesting trapper. I asked, "Did you ever hear the story about Caribou running from his cabin up the McGregor when he saw some women coming? Apparently they had something to do with the Monkman Pass Highway."

"Yes, I did hear that. He wouldn't have anything to do with women, you know. There's another good story about him that took place in Aleza Lake. There was this young Swede that lived there years ago — I can't remember his name now. Well, this guy came into some inheritance money somehow and went to town to do some partying. About two weeks later he came back with a woman and they were both pretty loaded up with booze. This guy lived a few miles from the town, so he took his friend and spent the night in a shed that belonged to Highways. The next morning he got up and found that his girlfriend was froze up hard as a board, as it had been very cold that night. Well, he took her over to the store and people that were in charge there wouldn't let him in, because they didn't know if there had been foul play or not, so he stood her up against the window, just like one of those store mannequins. Well he wasn't getting anywhere like that, so he took her over to Caribou's cabin and just threw her on his bunk. Now you know Caribou never had anything to do with a live woman so he sure wasn't going to stay there with a dead one. They say he came out of his chair and went out the door like the cabin was on fire. The police showed up after while, and I guess everything finally got back to normal when they found out that the woman had died of natural causes."

"I've heard that Caribou was excellent at handling a boat, is that true?"

"He was really one of the best. He could pole a boat right up against the current and that's not easy to do."

As the memories came flooding back, Ego really got going. "There's a story about Caribou that I really like. He was quite a smart man, you know. I mean he seemed to know a lot about medicine and things. He had a neighbour, a trapper named Frank Lehman that lived up the east fork, just below Eight-mile Canyon. Well, this guy had cleared a spot and planted a garden there and folks called it Garden Creek. Well, Frank and Caribou were walking along the river there and Frank was behind when a grizzly jumped out of the alders and grabbed Frank by the ass and knocked his gun flying. He shook him so hard that Caribou couldn't even shoot, even though Frank was hollering for him to shoot. When the bear let go and jumped back into the woods, Frank was mad at Caribou for not shooting, but Caribou said 'I couldn't, because I was afraid I'd hit you instead of the bear.' Then Frank got hold of his rifle and went back in the bush after the bear with Caribou telling him to leave it alone because he had enough already. Frank went back into the woods with blood spurting out of his ass and the bear heard him coming so it came back to meet him. It took three shots, but he stopped that bear and then they went back to his cabin where Caribou went to work on him. He collected some pitch from a balsam tree and heated it up on the stove, and then he put that on the wounds and I guess Frank hollered something awful. It must have hurt, you know, but a few weeks later he was up and around again and was okay."

When I left Ego's home that day, I remembered other stories I had heard about this colourful man called Caribou. Since then I have talked with several people who grew up around Aleza Lake and they have many nice things to say about him. Apparently it was a common sight to see his little cabin jammed full of teenagers while a bottomless coffee pot brewed on the stove. The young people were totally absorbed in his endless tales of adventures in the forests he loved so well. Almost all the young people there were taught to swim by this aged trapper who was like a fish in the water. Some of these people have described him as a teddy bear and a huggy bear and just the nicest person you could ever hope to meet. Caribou John will be remembered for many reasons, but I think the classic tale about him is the one where he was minding his own business at his cabin in Aleza Lake when the local mill boss approached him and asked if he would like to push logs up the jack ladder at the mill for a while. Well, he said he would think about it but he didn't like to rush into anything. The next thing you know, a local farmer asked him if he would like to help him make hay for a while. Caribou again said that he would think about it, then got into his boat and headed back up the McGregor River, where a man could have a little peace and quiet without being threatened with work.

Henry Hobi with dugout canoe at Fontiniko or Moose Creek. c.1935.

3

THE PRATHERS

IT WAS 1936 WHEN BILL RICHARDSON PURCHASED THE SLIM
Lake trapline from Fred Rankin, and it was about four years later
that my brother Clarence and I met Bill on the railway tracks. We
were just young shavers then and because Bill was a trapper,
we had him pegged right up there about two notches below God.
He was on his way to hunt moose, but stopped for a minute to talk
with us. We asked him if that was a good rifle he was carrying, and
he responded by pointing to a mountain several miles away and saying, "You see that mountain over there? Well I can shoot a moose
on that mountain right from here, but I have to remember to put lots
of salt on the bullet so that the meat will keep until I get there." He
walked away leaving us with the distinct impression that we had just
been in the presence of greatness. In fact, I figured he was probably
the best ever.

Our awe didn't last though; we happened to mention it to Dad
and he burst our bubble by telling us that this gentleman wasn't called
'Bullshit Bill' for nothing.

We had another episode with Bill about a year later when he came
to our farm to help butcher a cow. He had brought along his dog
which was well-known around the community as a cat killer, and Bill
was always ready to remind people of that fact. As they were busy
working on the cow, our cat came around the house into view.
Instantly upon seeing the dog, its fur puffed out and its tail appeared
about four times its normal size. Slowly and deliberately, one step at
a time, it approached the dog until about ten feet separated them.
The dog watched the cat's approach more puzzled than concerned,
but that's because it didn't have all the information.

He didn't know that just a couple of days earlier this cat had given
birth to kittens and that the kittens had been taken away. Now as they
stood staring at each other there could be no doubt: the cat had found

the kitten thief. For several minutes they stood staring at each other until something distracted the dog, making it turn its head. Then, like a steel spring releasing, the cat was on his back with 20 claws and a sharp set of teeth just a blur of activity. Out across the fields they went and when they disappeared from view, the cat was still in the saddle.

Whenever Bill came to visit after that, his dog would wait for him out at the edge of our farm. Try as we might, we were never able to coax it in. There was just no way he was going to fall for 'the old cat on the back trick' again.

Bill brought back stories of his adventures in the forests, but because he joked so much, no one knew when to believe him. In 1945 he sold the trapline and retired.

Now enters a sailor back from the war. In 1945, Oliver Prather, who lived in the community of Longworth, BC, bought Richarson's Slim Lake trapline and returned to the forests which had always been his first love. As a lad, he had spent a great deal of time trapping with his father and had learned a great deal about the forests from him.

One of Oliver's early memories concerned the time…Heck! I'll let him tell it:

"I was walking along my trapline and came face to face with a cougar. It snarled at me and then jumped right into a pile of down trees beside the trail. I was afraid to turn my back for fear it might jump me, so I took my little .22 calibre rifle and shot it in the head." Oliver shook his head as the memories returned and then continued, "I was darned lucky to kill that thing, if I had just wounded it the story could have been a lot different."

Many of Oliver's best memories of the wilderness concerned wolves. Like virtually all the trappers I talked with about wolves at the time when they were at their numerical peak in the 1930s and 1940s, Oliver felt that the wildlife people had to take action. The following description is of one of his finds. "I was walking along Boulder Creek, just west of Longworth, when I came upon some deer that had just been killed by wolves. The sign in the snow was real fresh and easy to read. I searched around and in just a small area I found 15 dead deer. They had all been killed in a short period of time, in one frenzied killing spree."

Oliver was one of many people who tried their luck at hunting wolves for their bounty. Just like many of the others, he learned just how wily and evasive they can be. In his 50 years in the forests, he got the grand total of four.

When I asked Oliver what the most memorable moment was from all his years of guiding and trapping he responded, "I was snowshoeing down Hungary Creek one night. Yes! I would have to say that was the best. I had my bug (candle in a tin can) with me but I hadn't bothered to light it because there was just enough moonlight to see by. I had my .22 rifle on my back at the time, but it turned out that it was no help. As I walked along, a large pack of wolves started howling right beside me. Right away my hair came up and lifted my toque a couple inches. I lit the bug as quick as I could but that didn't frighten them. Instead they escorted me along the trail for about one mile, sometimes in front, sometimes alongside or behind me." Oliver shook his head as he added, "Man! That combined howling went right through me. I was sure glad when they moved away and let my toque settle back down again."

Left to right: Ken Hooker, Oliver Prather, Jim Hooker, Jim Chambers and Catsy Hooker with 60-inch moose antlers.

I questioned Oliver about whether he had ever had any serious arguments with bears, as he had spent many years guiding, and this brought a smile to his face. "I recall the time I was taking an American hunter out for grizzly and we went to check the carcass of a moose he had taken earlier. When we got fairly close, the bear sensed our presence and let out a mighty roar. The hunter stopped dead in his tracks and said, 'Okay! That's good enough for me! I've got my money's worth! Let's go home!' We went home."

Once I got him onto the subject of bear, he added this story: "I remember the time I was walking through the ridges on a summer day when I came upon the remains of a moose with fresh grizzly sign all around. I looked up the draw where the moose had come down and could plainly see where the grizzly's claws had torn the bark off several trees. Either the grizzly had been on the moose's back, or else it had its front leg around the moose's neck because the sign plainly showed that it had been grabbing trees in an effort to stop. It obviously worked, because all the bones were piled up right at the bottom of the draw."

I asked Oliver what his closest brush with disaster had been and he continued: "That's easy! It was the time I took a hunter out for a mountain goat north of Pass Lake. I think it was 1957. We camped around timberline and then sat around the campfire on what was a perfect October evening. When we finally retired for the night it was beneath a clear moonlit sky. About four o'clock in the morning the tent poles collapsed and the tent fell on us. A foot of heavy wet snow had fallen and it was more than the support poles could bear. When I heard the poles breaking, I threw myself to the side and managed to free one arm. As soon as I got free, I went to help the hunter who was unable to move at all. I got him out from under that load of snow and thankfully he was all right, but it just goes to show you the endless bag of tricks that nature can have in store for people out there in the forests."

Oliver liked to reminisce about the beautiful Slim Lake Valley, about how he used to watch six to eight moose out in the water at the same time foraging on aquatic plants. The fishing was something right out of this world, and ospreys would circle and dive endlessly in their pursuit of fish. Up above, the eagles would circle while looking for an easy meal if they could steal it from the ospreys. Otherwise they were forced to dive down and get their own. Added to that were the howls of the wolf packs and the call of the loons that always made him feel that his home cabin area was about as close as he could get to a heaven on earth.

Oliver's father Orv Prather, was a woodsman in the old-fashioned style. One of the original Bear River (now the Bowron River) trappers, he gave real meaning to the word tough. Whenever Orv came to Penny, he would stop and visit with my father, and it didn't take long before they were lost in a another world with stories of wilderness adventures.

Orv Prather at his Driscoll Creek cabin, 1959.

On one visit to our home, Orv was telling Dad a story when he paused to light a cigarette. When he finished lighting the cigarette, he shook the match a few times and then put his hand down by his side. The match had not gone out; however, instead it kept burning all the way to the top while the flames licked up around his thumb and fingers. With my brother Clarence and I staring in disbelief, the match burned itself out, and only then did Orv shake his hand a few more times. Now if that isn't tough, I want someone to explain to me what tough is.

Like many other woodsmen who spent a lifetime in the woods, Orv had his run-in with grizzlies. "I was coming home off the trapline when I noticed a family of grizzly bears walking parallel to me on an adjacent ridge. I was on one ridge and they were on another. This was an unusual bear family because there was a yearling as well as two cubs. Now and then the mother would glance my way, but she seemed unconcerned. Suddenly, she led an attack straight at me and I had to put my .33 Winchester to work." With Dad almost leaning over the table in anticipation, Orv went on, "By the time I got my rifle ready, those bear were right up to me and I got away several shots at point-blank range and managed to stop them. By the time I finished them off, I was out of ammunition and pretty well shaken up."

According to Orv's son Oliver he was more than just a bit shaken up. Apparently when some men went back to the area to skin out the bears, Orv was not among them. Understandably he had endured enough excitement to last him for some time.

Orv's favorite dish on the trapline was macaroni and cheese, and this is what he set about making on his arrival at a line cabin he hadn't visited in some time. "I put the kettle on to boil, made the macaroni and cheese, and then sat down to eat. Well, I was eating away and all of a sudden I noticed a peculiar taste, but I kept eating until I ran into a bone. Now I knew damned well that there were no bones in macaroni and cheese so I started investigating. A few minutes later the riddle was solved when I found the remains of a mouse in the kettle." Orv looked around at all of us obviously enjoying the expressions on our faces, and then said, "For a minute or two there I thought I was going to get sick, then I decided, aw, what the hell! You're down there now, you might as well stay."

Probably the most priceless story I ever heard about Orv was told to me by Virgil Brandner who was a Forest Service patrolman at the time. A group of men had packed far into the forest to fight a wildfire that had been started by lightning. Toward evening, they set up a tent and then retired for the night. Shortly after they retired, a heavy rainstorm hit which lasted most of the night. When they arose the next morning, Orv, who talked to himself a lot, started mumbling about not being able to find his boots. Finally he opened the front of the tent to behold his boots standing in an upright position outside. Orv went out, dumped the rainwater out of his boots, and then said, "Why, you goddamned simple old fool. You've been in the woods for 60 years and you still haven't got enough sense to bring your boots in out of the rain." He paused for a few seconds and then added, "Oh well, you're young yet, you'll learn."

To paint a true picture of Orv, I would like to add a story that was told to me by a prospector named Harold Olson, also a resident of Longworth. I first met Harold while fighting a forest fire in 1958, when after a hard day's work, we sat around the campfire telling stories. Harold told us about a trip he had gone on with Orv and Oliver, when Oliver was just a lad of about eight. "It was late October, when after packing through the forests all day, we decided to camp for the night. I crawled into my sleeping bag and was almost asleep when I noticed young Oliver lying on the ground shivering uncontrollably. I called to him to come over and then managed to tuck him in the sleeping bag with me. Then I fell asleep. A short time after daybreak I awoke to an incredible sight: Orv was lying on the ground in his bone-dry pants and jacket, snoring contentedly while around him the ground was covered by a thick white frost. No matter how you look at it, there's just no way he should have survived the night." Harold paused for effect, then added, "When you slept out with Orv, the best shelter you could hope for was a big spruce tree and sometimes it wasn't the best of spruce at that." After a minute's silence, he again added, "Anywhere a moose could sleep, Orv could sleep too."

This prospector, Harold Olson, after spending a lifetime in the forests without having any problem with bears, was attacked and killed by a grizzly near Longworth, BC in September, 1971. He was cutting a trail through the forest to Toneko Lake when he failed to return home. The previous day, the bear had come to the home of Torsten Berg where it broke in the door and took a quarter of moose meat out of the porch. Torsten had been in Prince George at the time when he received a phone call from Bob McCoy, a neighbour, informing him of the break-in. He immediately returned to Longworth with his wife Ivy where after securing the house, he went to meet Harold. Part way along the trail, he got concerned that the bear might return to the house where Ivy was alone. This caused him to return home. When Harold had not returned by the following morning, Torsten's son Carl and a neighbour Ronald Turner went looking for him. Along the trail they found grizzly tracks, and then they came upon a fresh bear bed. Nearby they found Harold's body. It was in a near sitting position against a tree with one hand still holding part of the face and scalp that had been torn off by the bear's vicious attack. A length of rope that had been on Harold's pack was found wrapped around his legs. His axe lay nearby.

There is a footnote to this story that I feel deserves telling. About seven years prior to this attack a brown grizzly bear was wounded by hunters in the mountains just east of Longworth. The bear managed to escape. Several times in the following years, a large brown boar grizzly roared out his hatred at the first scent of man. I personally experienced this mad roaring and I can state that it gave me the creeps, to say the least. During the month of May following Harold's death I was with a man named Gordon Ross when he shot a big grizzly just three miles from the spot where Harold was killed. We were hiding behind a couple small trees 200 yards downwind of a train-killed moose when just before dark, we heard something heavy coming through the forest. It was the grizzly returning to the moose carcass that it had almost entirely consumed in the two previous nights. When it reached the right-of-way opening I expected it to stop, look and listen, as bears almost always do while scenting the air to make sure no surprises await them. Instead this bear came right out like it owned the entire area.

Gordon took the bear hide to Prince George taxidermist Al Rand who thoroughly examined it and found a neck injury compatible with an axe cut. Since Harold was such an experienced woodsman, I think there is a real good chance that he may have struck the bear a blow with the axe. And I also want to state that we never saw or heard this brown boar grizzly though we have been in these mountains every year since that time. I realize there is no way to be certain, but I think there is a darned good chance that Gord got a man-killer.

4

PENNY

WHEN THE GRAND TRUNK PACIFIC RAILWAY REACHED Penny in 1913, Mr. and Mrs. John McPherson were among the first pioneer settlers to arrive there. As this was the end of steel at that time, they were forced to spend the winter there and so it became their home for many years. John got together with a few Chinese gentlemen that were laid off the railway construction jobs, and they spent a considerable amount of time cutting a trail through the mountains to Barkerville, a distance of almost 60 miles. John then spent several years prospecting in the Barkerville area and commuting between there and Penny where his family lived.

Ben and Adelia Sykes had already arrived there, having come down the Fraser River from Tête Jaune in 1912 with their three children. During those early years, Adelia kept a diary, starting it in August 1912 and continuing it until May 1915. Because the Sykes family played such an important part in the area, I will start with some excerpts from her diary to give an accurate description of what life was like at that time. Also the excerpts show how much these people were forced to live off the land and trade with each other. The numbers mentioned, 53, 66, and so on refer to mileages along the Grand Trunk Pacific Railroad. The often-mentioned 'birds' were grouse, and the 'water rabbits' were beavers. I begin Adelia's diary:

AUGUST 19, 1912: We left Sandcreek at 10.45. Stayed at 53 (Tête Jaune) a few minutes. Had dinner at 1. Got to 66, stayed all night. Got there about 2 and got in groceries.

AUGUST 20: Left 66 at 8.30. Sun shines, everything fine. Had dinner at Murrays. Went up a slough looking for ducks and rested awhile. Went through death rapids a-flying. 4 o'clock, passed the big steamer. Camped on Beaver River all night. Got 2 birds, 1 rabbit. Lots of mosquitoes.

AUGUST 21: Started at 8.30, sun shines. Everything lovely. Saw one canoe at 83. Had dinner on an island. Stayed all night at Garnet Creek. Got traps and saw geese.

AUGUST 22: Started fine. Passed game warden at 114. We walked a half mile through woods. Ben and Harry went through rapids. Had dinner below rapids. Passed gasoline boat in Moose Canyon. Struck a rock, did not hurt boat. Camped all night in old campground. Rained all night.

AUGUST 23: Started and went aways, but had to stop, the fog was too thick. Burns Meat boat went by while we were waiting. Raining again. Got 1 bird, 12 o'clock the conveyor [Sternwheeler *SS Conveyor*] went by. 1.30 got dinner at 133. Got to the mill, stayed all night, had supper. Breakfast at Cullens. Raining some.

AUGUST 26: Started downriver at 10.45. Camped and got two ducks, got dinner, dried bedding, put up hammock. Alice is sleeping in it. Put up tent.

Mr. and Mrs. John McPherson. They lived in Penny, BC from 1913 to 1930. He cut a trail to Barkerville where he prospected during the First World War.

AUGUST 27: Clear morning. Ben went up for salmon. I wrote two letters. Saw some tracks down about 2 o'clock, looks like moose tracks. Saw three boats going down. Heard five shots, about 5:30 heard three more shots. Ben got home six o'clock. Got 1 salmon, about 4-5 pounds and one duck.

AUGUST 28: Bright morning. Sold some traps. Went up to mill and got some groceries. Posted two letters and had dinner at Cullens. Came home. Raining a little. Sold some tobacco and got supper. Bird flew over tree, shot her, fell right by supper, built fire, to bed.

AUGUST 29: Raining again. Shot 3 birds before breakfast. Clear again. Started downriver at 12:30. Sold rubber shoes, got bread, went to Dome Creek, stayed all night. Rained in the night.

AUGUST 31: Left Dome Creek. Saw Daniel's boat. Got dinner at Bill Rover's camp. Rained hard while there. Started downriver again. Big boat passed us below Slim Creek. Camped on left side. Stayed all night.

SEPTEMBER 2: Sun shines. Did some washing, put bedding in the sun. Had dinner. Ben went down to camp, traded 1 bottle of brandy for 9 big cans of milk, 7 lbs. butter, 4 lbs. cheese, about $9.00 worth. Sun shines all day.

SEPTEMBER 3: Sun up high. Ben went hunting but only got 1 bird. Cleared ground, felled trees, started house.

SEPTEMBER 4: Sun shines, worked on house. 4 scows passed by. Dog smelt something on the other side. After supper went to bed.

SEPTEMBER 5: Sun shines. Ben went down to Cranberry Marsh. Maybe seen moose. Got back, went up river, got a big piece of bear. Lots of fat. Got 1 bird.

SEPTEMBER 6: Fried out fat, got three gallons. Then worked on house. Then made dutch oven and had supper.

SEPTEMBER 7: Fine day. Went hunting, Got 6 birds with five shots, shot two heads off at once. Had dinner. Worked on house the rest of day. Saw moose tracks while hunting.

SEPTEMBER 9: Cloudy again. Went over river and cut big cedar tree. Got half enough lumber to cover our roof. Brought it over in canoe. While there Ben shot 1 bird and I shot 2 ducks in the river. Had dinner, had my picture taken on canoe with ducks and gun, then worked on house.

SEPTEMBER 12: Fine day. Had breakfast. Ben went hunting, got a big black bear, got home at 4.30. Sold hide at camp. Got 2 loaves of bread. Skinned meat, got supper, went to bed at dark.

SEPTEMBER 13: Sun up, had breakfast, going to work on house. Moved in house today.

SEPTEMBER 14: Fine day. Worked on house. Eight scows went by, one gasoline and some little boats. After dinner went over river, got some lumber, made table, traded bear meat for pepper, potatoes, flour and milk.

SEPTEMBER 26: Raining some. Shot 2 geese in slough.

OCTOBER 5: Foggy morning. Ben went to look at traps. Got 2 water rabbits. Got one pail jam, 8 lbs. butter, 1 lb. chocolate.

OCTOBER 11: Ben went up to slough. Set some traps after dinner. We all went to look at some grizzly bear tracks on sand, close to cabin. Coming back shot 3 birds by cabin. Ben shot 1 bird more.

Ada Sykes, coming in from duck hunting.

OCTOBER 12: Fine day. Ben set and baited 54 traps. Caught 1 mink. I washed some. Gave children a bath. 1 bird.

OCTOBER 13: Sunday again. Two scows went by, they gave us 1 pail of jam, 4 big tins of milk, 4 lbs. bacon. Ben went to Elmers.

OCTOBER 21: Fine day. We went over river and cut cedar tree, got lumber for floor and porch. Scows went by, gave us a lot of groceries.

NOVEMBER 2: Ben went with Dr. Gray and Mr. McDougall hunting on the mountains. They stayed all night.

NOVEMBER 3: Sunday again. Snowed 3 inches in night. Ben and men got home. They paid him $15.00. The scows gave him $35.00 groceries.

NOVEMBER 6: Nice morning. Ben went to look at traps in slough. Got 1 otter, 1 water rabbit, 1 weasel, 11 muskrat. 4 men stayed to dinner. Afternoon got 1 rat.

NOVEMBER 8: Ben started on trapline, saw moose, shot him with manser [Mauser rifle]. Sold quarter for $10.00.

NOVEMBER 9: Nice day. Ben looked at traps in slough. Got 1 weasel, 1 big eagle measured 7 1/2 feet from wing to wing.

NOVEMBER 11: Fine day. Ben went on south trapline. Got 9 weasels, 1 marten, 4 caribou shot with manser (Mauser rifle) on the dead gallop.

THE FOREGOING IS JUST A SAMPLE OF THE DAILY LIFE OF THE Sykes family. The mention of an eagle with a seven and one-half foot wingspan is obviously a golden eagle, many of which were to be seen in the mountains during the first years I went there. The $15 received from Dr. Gray and Mr. McDougal for taking them hunting in the mountains was the start of a guiding career for Ben.

At the same time, there were several others around the area who were to play an important part during the early years. There was a trapper named Fred Rankin who had trapped in the area as early as 1910. As well, there was John and Morgan Narboe, both guides and trappers, who seemed to have a stormy relationship with bears.

Within a short time, Ben Sykes and John Narboe both got into guiding in a big way, as John had been a famous guide in the Kootenays before his arrival at Penny and had brought his clientele with him. They were two of the early guides on the McGregor River, and later in the mountains around Penny, where most of the following stories took place.

One of the hunters whom John Narboe had known when he guided in the Kootenays was L. A. Robinson, traffic manager of the New York Central Railway. In a hunt up the McGregor River, Mr. Robinson was being guided by Sykes and Narboe when he got the biggest grizzly bear seen up to that time. The bear measured eight feet six inches in length, and six feet wide at the narrowest point.

This Mr. Robinson was also a guest of Ben Sykes a few years later when they had an interesting moment with some grizzlies. Mr. Robinson was taking movies of a mother and cubs when the mother became aware of his presence. She attacked and he threw his hat downhill toward her to create a diversion, while at the same time he told Ben not to shoot. The hat struck the bear a glancing blow on

Ben Sykes, one of the original McGregor River guides. c. 1920.

the head just as she was standing upright and it was captured on film. The bear then turned and led her cubs away.

My dad saw the film later and said it looked as though the bear was posing with a hat on.

Ben Sykes had an experience to remember when he took a friend of Mr. Robinson's on a hunt back into the mountains. After a couple of days in the forest, this man told Ben to get him out to civilization at once or he would have a crazy man on his hands. This person had been raised in New York City and had known only continuous noise all his life. The silence overwhelmed him.

My dad used to pack supplies into the mountains for Ben's guiding camps, and it was then that the story of Snowshoe Bill originated. Snowshoe Bill, so named because of the huge tracks that he left, was supposedly a grizzly bear that roamed the mountains to the north of the community, and throughout the years he just kept on growing in size. Even many years later, Dad kept these memories alive and would come home with stories about how Snowshoe Bill had been here or there — done this or that, and it was the kind of thing that children can build dreams around. It may well have played a large part in the tremendous love and fascination that I have always felt for the wilderness.

Into this web of woodsmen, came a trapper named Charlie Hartsell, who, because he was an American, could not buy a trapline. He put up the money to buy the Slim Lake trapline in Fred Rankin's name and became a silent partner.

During the fall of 1919, Charlie Hartsell was attempting to drive a moose through the forest to a waiting hunter when he was shot by the hunter who mistook him for the moose. The bullet hit him in the arm, went through and struck him in the side. Somehow, he survived, and eventually returned to the trapline.

In the meantime, Morgan Narboe went missing while fishing at Slim Lake. A search turned up the empty canoe caught against the shore of the lake. His body was recovered in six feet of water. It was assumed that he had suffered a cardiac arrest because he was such an excellent swimmer no one could believe that he had drowned. This occurred just below the narrows in Slim Lake, and to this day that spot is known as Morgan's Hole. Morgan was buried right beside the original cabin at Slim Lake.

For several years, John Narboe trapped with Charlie Hartsell at Slim Lake, and Charlie soon found out that John had a thing about bears — he just couldn't leave them alone. Charlie was convinced that John would be killed by a bear someday.

Together, they shot a moose one fall and carried some of it back to the cabin for food, the rest they left as bait to try to get a big fat grizzly bear for their winter lard supply. A big grizzly moved on the remains, but it was too clever to hunt, so John changed tactics and prepared a gun-set, hoping that the bear would shoot itself if it moved the bait.

The next day, Charlie was fishing a few miles away along the lake when he heard the set-gun fire. As he had his rifle with him, he headed back along the lake, knowing that John would need this rifle to go in and check the gun-set. About half-way back, he was surprised to hear another shot reverberate through the valley. He kept paddling and got back to the cabin just in time to see John emerge from the forest with his own rifle in his hands. He then learned that John had been in the cabin when the set-gun went off and had rushed through the woods to find the grizzly lying wounded; he had then untied the rifle and finished it off, seemingly oblivious to the perilous position he would have been in had the set-gun wounded a cub or yearling.

John had another close brush with tragedy when he trailed a wounded grizzly into thick brush. The bear attacked, and just as it ran into him, he shot it in the neck. Together they went over a down tree with the bear landing right on top of him — stone dead. A short time later he arrived back at the cabin covered with blood. At first glance, Charlie thought his partner had been mauled but there was not a scratch on him anywhere.

The winter of 1920 saw the death of colourful old woodsman.

After the death of John Narboe, Charlie got his old time trapping partner Fred Rankin to assist him on the Slim Lake trapline, and these two men had something in common — a very healthy respect for grizzly bears. Late one fall, these two men set a bear trap on moose remains less than one-half mile from their main cabin, hoping to get a real fat bear to supply them with lard for cooking. That same evening just before midnight they were awakened by the roaring of a mad bear, that carried on all through the night, quieting down just before dawn.

Daylight found the two trappers paddling their canoe along the lake with their trusty 30-30s by their sides. When they spotted the grizzly, it was standing up, holding the trap right in front of its face, studying it just like a person would do. Both men took aim and fired — almost tipping the canoe over in the process. Instantly, they noticed that one bullet had struck the toggle chain, setting the bear free. As the big grizzly lunged for cover, the two trappers turned the canoe around and headed back toward the cabin with their trusty 30-30s by their sides.

Back at the cabin, the two men finally mustered up enough courage to go back along the lake for another look, where they found the bear dead. The other bullet had hit it in the neck, killing it almost instantly. Many, many times through the years, Mr. Rankin told us that this grizzly was 10 feet long.

During the Depression, my father was unemployed. As Charlie had quit the trapline, Mr. Rankin asked Dad if he would like to run trapline for him. Dad jumped at the chance, and then spent the winters of '30 to '33, running the line while Mr. Rankin stayed at the main cabin and took care of the fur.

One evening while Dad and I were sitting around the house talking about his days on the trapline. I asked, "What did you and Mr. Rankin talk about up there on the trapline on those long winter nights?"

Dad gave me a look of complete disbelief and said, "Talk? Huh! How are you going to talk to a man that knows everything." He paused for a minute and then added, "He had his books and stayed on his side of the cabin and I had my books and I stayed on my side of the cabin and that worked out fine."

"You must have had some misunderstandings at times, didn't you?' I asked.

"Yes. I remember one morning when I got up and made breakfast — as I usually did, and I made two large pancakes, one for me and one for him. I sat down to eat my pancake and it tasted kind of funny. I looked around and figured out that I had put baking soda in the batter instead of baking powder. Well, I got it down and then started gathering up some trapping supplies as I wanted to go to the top end of the lake to put out some beaver sets. Just as I went out the door of the cabin, Fred was getting dressed. I finished gathering up the things I needed and was just pushing the canoe off the shore when something whizzed by my ear and landed with a splash in the water right beside the canoe. I looked and there was the other pancake with one bite missing from it. I looked around just in time to see Fred step back in and close the cabin door. That evening when I came back to the cabin, I thought he was going to mention it, but instead he gave me a few days of silence."

Fred Rankin.
c. 1920.

After each trip around the line, Dad would spend a few days at the main cabin with Mr. Rankin and sooner or later they would have a few discussions. Like the evening...

"I went out to the toilet that night and when I came back in I told Fred there was a ring around the moon and that we might get a snowstorm. Well he said that he had just read in a science magazine that the moon didn't have anything to do with the weather. So that was all right, but a few days later he came in from the toilet and said that there was a full moon out there and that we were going to get a change in the weather. Well right away I told him that science says that the moon has nothing to do with the weather and he went Hurrummph and I kept quiet for a few days after that."

"What about that fishing story you used to tell?" I asked, hoping to get him going.

"That was in the late fall and Fred wanted to get some fish before winter set in. I didn't give a darn about fishing, but I told him that I would paddle the boat if he wanted to fish and he sure went for that. We went out on the lake and he started fishing with a piece of weight and a hook on the end of a piece of string. We fished there for a while and then I saw a great big fish off to the side of the boat. I pointed it out to Fred and just then that fish made a pass at the hook. It came right up to the hook and then looked at it and swam away. You know, when that fish was coming to the hook I looked and Fred's legs were shaking like a leaf. Can you imagine a 50 year-old man shaking because of a fish? What's the matter with a fellow like that, anyway?"

I didn't answer, Dad wouldn't have understood.

Like so many others that spent a lot of time alone, my dad used to talk to himself, and he once offered an interesting observation as to why. He felt that when a person spends a great deal of time in complete silence that they need to hear the sound of a human voice, even if it's just their own. The old saying that a person who talks to himself is crazy, was obviously formed without much thought. It is nothing more or less that thinking out loud.

Of all the stories Dad told about his days in the forests, I think my favorite was this: "It was an evening in late fall when I arrived at a line cabin after a long days walk through the forest. I ate my evening meal and skinned out the fur and then I decided to go to bed. It was fairly warm in the cabin when I went to bed, so I just pulled the blankets up to my waist and blew out the candle. Outside the cabin the wind was howling in the trees and you know that makes it kind of spooky. Later on, it started cooling off in the cabin so I pulled the blankets up to my neck. Then a queer thing happened. Something started pulling the blankets down again. I was half asleep when that happened, but by the time they got down to my waist, I was wide awake. I grabbed them and pulled them back up again, then held them and listened, but all I could hear was the sound of the wind in the trees. After a minute, I let go of the blankets and they started down again. Now that was too much. I jumped out of the bunk, lit a match, and peered under the bunk, and there was the ghost. It was only a piece of board with a nail in one end. When I pulled the blankets up it lifted off the floor, then when I let go, the weight of the board pulled them down again. For a few minutes there, I was ready to take my chances out in the woods."

A neat place name originated when my dad and Fred Rankin decided to try cutting a trail from Slim Lake into the upper Liverson (now Centennial) Creek area. About three quarters of a mile from where Slim Creek exits Tumuch Lake, a creek enters the lake. They followed this creek due west, cutting trail as they went through some hellish tough going and steep slopes until they finally decided to give up and turn back, saying that only a crazy man would go that way. Well, the name stuck, and to this day that stream is known as "Crazy Man's Creek."

Another place-name story originated in the '20s, when a bachelor named Jean Delare decided to walk from Penny into Slim Lake to catch a good supply of fish. Walking along the 14 miles of the old Slim Lake trail, he misjudged the distance and was forced to spend the night under a big spruce tree that grew beside the trail. For many years after, this spot was known to forest travellers as "Jean Delare's Hotel."

There's another story about Jean Delare that begs telling. He lived in a cabin on the bank of the Fraser River in Penny, and not having an indoor toilet, was forced to answer nature's call by going outside, be it day or night. One night when the river was in flood stage, Jean felt the urge to go out and take a leak. Like many other people of his time, Jean had a cellar under his cabin in which to store vegetables during the winter. This night when he felt the urge, he swung his feet over the side of the bunk and tried to stand up. Instead, the rising flood waters had floated the cellar door away and he found himself down in the cellar filled with ice-cold Fraser River snowmelt. He was only down there for a short period of time, but rumour has it that he did a lot more than just take a leak while he was there.

One trapline story that Dad used to tell concerned wolves, and I think it is just another example that shows the intelligence of these beasts. "We had a pack of wolves that used to make their rounds and I noticed that they liked to cross the creek in the same place all the time. One day I went and took a closer look and I noticed that the reason they were crossing at that spot was because there were several rocks in the water there. Maybe you know that wolves don't like to get their feet wet any more that other animals, especially in the winter," Dad said, then continued. "Well, I saw that these wolves were stepping from one rock to the next, so I removed one of the rocks and put the tongue of the trap just level with the top of the water. The next trip around the line, well, there was this big wolf caught in the trap. You know, we left that trap set there for years but we never caught another wolf. I guess you can't fool them the same way twice."

Another story he used to tell was…"I was camped up Liverson Creek while trapping beaver one spring and I remember it was a real warm evening. I had a campfire going and when I got tired, I pulled my two woolen blankets over me and went to sleep. About four hours later I woke up because something was pressing down on me. It had snowed about one foot of heavy snow and my campfire was out. Well, I'm telling you, that was a pretty sad home. But I always kept birch bark and kindling ready, so about 10 minutes later I had a roaring fire going and everything looked like home again."

Since moose meat was an essential part of the winter food supply, my dad was elected to help get one. Out he went, on a November hunt that turned out to be much more than he bargained for. "I went out hunting and I got a shot at a moose through the trees, but I didn't hit it quite right, so it ran away. I followed its trail in the snow for half an hour and when I caught up to it, I found it dead in a creek. I took off my snowshoes and jumped in the water and started butchering it. I worked there for a while and suddenly I felt a chill go right through me, and then I knew I was in trouble. I climbed out of the creek and put my snowshoes on, and then I headed back to the cabin as fast as I could go."

"Did you really think you were in trouble?" I asked.

"I've never had a feeling like that. I figured I was in big trouble all right. As soon as I got in the cabin, I went to bed and covered up with all the blankets, but I just kept getting colder. Well, I knew that wasn't working so I jumped out of bed and boiled some water, and then I found a half-bottle of Minard's liniment, so I mixed that in about two quarts of water and drank it down just as hot as I could stand it. Then I went back under the blankets again and in about an hour I was sweating to beat hell. You know, in a couple hours the bed was soaking wet and I knew that I was all right. The next day I went back and dragged that moose out of the creek and brought some of it back to the cabin."

While it was well known that Dad had waterproofed boots that he always wore in the forest, what wasn't known is that he had water-proofed socks as well. Dad had a special formula that consisted of neats-foot oil and bear grease and he used to heat this mixture in a gallon can until it reached about 170 degrees F. He would then take this mixture and pour his boots full. After a few minutes, it would start coming through and we knew the boots were waterproofed. When Dad first used these boots after the 'treatment,' the first pair of socks came out black and totally waterproof. It was the need to replenish the bear grease for his 'formula' that led to the next story.

It started one day when an elderly homesteader named Dick Finer came to Dad with the information that he had found a freshly dug bear den. As this was September, Dad suggested they wait until after the snow came to go to its den and drive it out. Well the time went by, the snow arrived, and the two intrepid hunters went to the den site. Dick put his ear to the entrance and listened, then replied, "It's in there, Joe, I can hear it." While Dick stood guard with the rifle,

Dad went and cut a long pole, then proceeded to stick it down the hole and thrash it about. Suddenly Dick hollered, "It's coming, Joe, I can hear it." While the two men stood waiting in anticipation, gun at the ready, a porcupine emerged from the den.

Whether he was trapping or packing supplies for guides, Dad never carried a gun in the forest unless he was hunting, as he felt he had enough to carry without one. For this reason he had to use a stick or axe handle to dispatch trapped animals. This led to the following story:

"I remember the time that I caught a wolverine and gave it a few real good licks on the head. I put it in my packsack and went on along the trail. All of a sudden that bugger came back to life and I'm telling you we had a good fight out there. I've never seen anything so tough in my life."

"Do you think they're the toughest animal in the forest, Dad?"

"You bet. I sure wouldn't want to meet anything tougher," he added.

When Dad first started trapping at Slim Lake, he noticed that there was a shortage of marten. Since there was an abundance of squirrels, their main source of food, he thought it was rather strange that there was a shortage of marten. He checked the records and found that a few years earlier the trappers had caught 155 marten, then the next year had caught 55 marten, and the third year had caught only two. They had trapped it out.

In the spring of '33, Dad quit the trapline and Charlie Hartsell decided to return. As he and Fred Rankin were getting on in years, they hired a young Polish immigrant to run the line for them while they stayed at the main cabin at Slim Lake. They spent some time with him, teaching him how to set traps and then when they felt comfortable that he could handle the job, sent him up past T-Hell-N-Gone (now Shandy) Lake. With him, he carried a five-day supply of food. Two days after he left, a heavy snowstorm moved in and dropped several feet of snow on the area. In the days that followed it continued to snow. After a week had elapsed and he had not returned, the trappers knew he was in serious trouble. They almost exhausted themselves by keeping the trail open up past the head of

Tumuch Lake, a distance of about five miles in the direction he would have to come back from.

On the morning of the ninth day, they set off along the trail again in the hopes of meeting him and helping him back to the cabin. They only went about a quarter of a mile and they came upon his frozen body lying in the trail. They backtracked for some distance and found that he had been following the trail they had kept open, but where he came from or what happened to him was a mystery. He must have been in a state of extreme exhaustion for they found where he had hung his rifle in a tree on the bank of Crazy Man's Creek. He had continued on until he hit the bay about one mile from the main cabin. From here he could have seen the lights of the cabin if the two trappers were still up. Obviously totally exhausted, he decided to walk across the bay rather than follow the snowshoe trail around the bay. A layer of water and snow covered the ice, so he had gone just a short distance before his snowshoes loaded up and became unbearably heavy. He had taken them off, stood them up so he could find them later, and then had continued on across the bay. After finding the snowshoe trail again, he had carried on toward the cabin about 600 yards away. A couple hundred yards further on, he had arrived at a spot where a tree leaned heavily over the trail. Forced to get down on his hands and knees to crawl under the tree, he no longer had the strength to stand again. In this position the trappers found him, a victim of the cruel destiny that allowed him to die 400 yards from help because his only means of summoning that help — his rifle — hung uselessly in a tree a couple miles away.

Now the two elderly trappers were in one hell of a fix. They had to get out to notify the police, yet between them and Penny lay 14 miles of deep snow.

Early the next morning they started out breaking trail, continued on until after noon, and then headed back for Slim Lake. They had not reached the halfway point and were already thoroughly exhausted, yet knew they must get through the next day before more snow fell. They were on the trail again before daylight and by noon were already played out. They kept plodding on, though, taking turns breaking trail and when they were forced to rest, making certain they did not fall asleep. Late that evening they reached a home on the edge of the settlement of Penny, so exhausted that Charlie had to stay there for two days until he got enough strength to walk the short distance to his home.

The next morning two police officers arrived by train and began the snowshoe trip toward Slim Lake. That same evening they returned with broken snowshoes, having lost the trail as well as their enthusiasm.

One policeman returned to Prince George while the other, Constable George Soles, stayed. He asked the local storekeeper — Halvor Mellos — if he knew who might be able to assist him in finding the body. Halvor suggested he approach my father who had trapped the area previously. George set out to visit my dad, and this led to a rather humorous incident. About halfway along the trail to our home lived the Michaylenkos family who, like many others during the Depression, had some moonshine brewing. Sam happened to glance out the window to behold a policeman coming up the path so he turned to his daughter Nettie and said, "It's the police, quick, take the moonshine out and throw it down the toilet!" While Nettie hurried out the back door with the moonshine, Sam slowly walked over to answer the front door. "Sorry to bother you," said the policeman, "but I was wondering if it would be all right if I used your toilet?" On his way out to the toilet, George met Nettie on her way back with the empty container. On his way back through the house after he had finished his business, George thanked Sam, gave him a little wink, and then continued on his way with a more than obvious grin of satisfaction on his face.

Arriving at our home, George asked Dad if he would accompany him to Slim Lake, and Dad agreed. The *Prince George Citizen* of January 4th 1934, stated:

Onufry Lewoniak Died on Trail From Exposure
Became Exhausted on Trip to
Get a Supply of Fish and Froze to Death
POLICE BURY THE BODY
Victim was Within Half Mile of His Camp
When Played Out and Fell in Snow

The provincial police have satisfied themselves as to the circumstances surrounding the death of Onufry Lewoniak, whose body was found some days ago about half a mile from a trapper's cabin on Slim Lake, about eighteen miles south of Penny, on the CNR. News of the finding of the body was brought to Prince George on December 26th, and the matter of investigating the circumstances surrounding the same fell to Constables Soles and Murray. They made Penny on the evening of that day, and on the morning of December 27th commenced their hike to Slim Lake. There were three and one-half feet of light snow on the ground, the temperature stood at 42 degrees below zero, and they were forced to break the trail. When they had negotiated nine miles of the trail Constable Murray had the bad luck to break one of his snowshoes, and one of his feet becoming frozen the officers were forced to return to Penny.

On the morning of the 29th Constable Soles picked up Joe Boudreau as a guide and started south again for the lake, reaching it the following day, and locating the body of Lewoniak. He satisfied himself that death was due to misadventure and exposure, and the body was buried near the edge of the lake.

In his investigation Constable Soles learned the deceased and Charles Hartsell had been shacking for the winter with Fred Rankin, who was working a trapline in the vicinity of Slim Lake. On the morning of December 16th the grub in the shack was running low and Lewoniak decided to make a trip to the other end of the lake and catch some fish. When he failed to return to the cabin Rankin started out to look for him and came across the body face down in the snow. Lewoniak was evidently on his way back to the cabin when he played out. He had travelled through the slush on the top of the lake until his snowshoes became too heavy for him. He had then taken them off and stood them on end, deciding to make the rest of the journey without them. He was evidently at the end of his reserve strength for a short distance from where he left the snowshoes he dropped in the trail and was frozen to death.

Little is known of Lewoniak other than that he was a Pole and was 35 years old. He drifted into Prince George with other unemployed men and identified himself with their organization.

IT IS INTERESTING TO NOTE THAT ACCORDING TO THE POLICE report neither Charlie nor Onufry were trapping. The reason for this discrepancy lies in the fact that neither man had a trapper's licence, lack of which, upon conviction, could have netted the men up to six months in jail. The story about going away to catch fish was fabricated because there was excellent fishing right beside the main cabin door in Slim Lake.

My dad told us that there was three feet of snow on the body which they had to remove, then another four feet beneath that, and then they still had to dig the grave. He said that was one job he was damned glad to be done with. Whenever he told this story, Dad would always add a touch of humour to it by telling us that when they were digging the grave, George asked him, "Say Joe, does it bother you to be around a dead body?" "No!" Dad responded, "I've never had any trouble with them, I've found it's the live bodies you've got to watch."

After Dad had returned to Penny, he went to visit Fred Rankin, and they spent some time discussing what may have happened to the young trapper. They agreed it was most likely that he had got turned around in the blizzard in an area where there were two creeks just a short distance apart that flowed in different directions. If he had followed the wrong creek, he may have walked for a day or more before realizing his error.

Realizing that he was getting too old to tramp the forests, Mr. Rankin sold the line in 1936 and retired in Penny on the bank of the creek that still bears his name. As Mr. Rankin and Dad were fellow trappers, it was only natural that we would think of him at Christmas time, and so a tradition was born. Every Christmas Day we would take a large platter of turkey with all the trimmings, a large bowl of Mom's homemade chicken-noodle soup, and a bowl of pudding with sauce over to his cabin, where we would find him at the door waiting for us.

One festive season we were sitting around the house on Boxing Day when Mom suddenly exclaimed, "Oh my gosh! We forgot Mr.

Rankin yesterday." She quickly got some food together and we took it to his cabin where he met us at the door with, "I waited for you people all day until late last night and then I realized you weren't coming." The hurt in his voice was obvious, and only then did we fully realize just how much this had come to mean to him through the years.

Probably the most important thing in his life after he left the trapline, was his hobby of amateur astronomy, and he spent many a clear night gazing into the heavens.

There were three things in life that Fred Rankin didn't trust — grizzlies, banks, and hospitals — and he did his level best to stay clear of all three of them.

His first love was his pipe, which spent a large portion of the day in his mouth. His second love was astronomy, and I would have to say that his third love was moose liver. Anytime we got a moose, we would take a good sized piece of liver over to him. Each time he would ask us, "When was that animal shot?" His reason for asking was that he had once become deathly ill from eating moose liver, and he blamed it on eating the liver only a couple of hours after the moose had been killed.

In his later years when his legs could no longer carry him, we would get his groceries for him from the general store, and I sure remember the first time I did. I stopped in at his cabin and asked if he needed anything from the store, whereupon he handed me a grocery list. Just as he was turning around, I asked, "Do you want these groceries put on your bill?" — as it was common to do in those days. He whirled around like I had stabbed him in the back with a knife, and said, "Bill? What bill? I don't owe anybody anything!" He then turned around again and went to get cash, leaving me quite humbled for daring to suggest that he owed money.

After I had brought his groceries and mail back to the cabin for him, we sat around talking, and I put a question to him that had troubled me for some time: I asked why many old-timers cut off their own frozen toes or splinted their own fractured bones rather than go to medical attention.

In between puffs on his pipe he answered, "Well, when your friends go to the hospital and don't come back, you start to get suspicious."

Not trusting banks, he kept his money in some strange places. For instance he kept $4000 in a baking-powder can right on his table. The original coupon was left on top of the money so that it looked and felt like a full can of powder. Only after his death when the cabin was being cleaned up, was it discovered.

My brother Clarence, who owned the property on which Mr. Rankin's cabin was situated, lived just a stone's throw away, so this led to a close friendship between them. Often he would visit Mr. Rankin in the evenings and could not help but notice him develop a great sense of humour in his later years.

Just as he was leaving the cabin one fall evening, Clarence remarked that he was going to go home and take a bath. This prompted Mr. Rankin to come back with, "Yes, I think I'll take a bath too one of these days toward spring when it warms up a little more."

When asked how he felt he would sometimes reply, "I don't give a damn how I feel."

Another expression of his was, "When I die I'm going to buy a Cadillac and drive all over hell."

One evening when Clarence stopped in to check on him, Mr. Rankin said, "You know, a funny thing happened around here today. I fried an egg for breakfast and when I was carrying it over to the table it slipped off the plate and fell on the floor. Well I looked for that thing for over an hour and couldn't find it. But that was all right, because I finally found it this afternoon, so I had it for supper."

My favorite story about Mr. Rankin happened the day he got a visit from an elderly friend named Dick Finer. During the visit Fred asked Dick if he would like a cup of tea. Dick assured him that he did, then watched as Fred walked to the table and inspected a few cups that had been placed upside down there. Finally not sure that the cup he selected was clean enough, he walked over to where a drying line hung over the cookstove, pulled down a wool sock that had been drying there, and wiped out the cup. When someone asked, "Did you drink it?" He replied, "Yes! I drank it all right, but it sure went down hard."

When Rankin's health gave out and he wouldn't go to the hospital, the police had to get involved. Clarence told the police that he kept a loaded handgun under his pillow, so it was agreed that Clarence should go in first and get it — which he did. When the police entered and told Mr. Rankin that he had to go to the hospital, he said, "All right, but I want to get a few things first." He then walked over and stuck his hand in under the pillow — finding that the gun was gone — he went peacefully.

While in the hospital he found that his fears were unfounded. In fact he couldn't believe how well he was treated. Nursed back to health, he returned to his cabin where he stayed until he got gangrene in his left leg. This time there was no problem getting him to go to the hospital.

A couple of weeks later, Clarence went to visit him in the hospital and found him near death. In a voice barely above a whisper, he said, "You came too late!"

A few days later in the McBride Hospital, Mr. Rankin strapped on his snowshoes for the last time and broke trail to that great trapline in the hereafter: where the fur is never rubbed, the snow never gets sticky, and all the fur traders are honest.

5

HUMOUR

MY PARENTS JOE AND BESSIE BOUDREAU ARRIVED IN PENNY, BC on May 15, 1923. After several moves, Mom said that she was tired of it and that she wanted to build a home. In 1926, they took out a pre-emption on a one-quarter section of land in a beautiful little valley with a stream running through it. On the hillside there was a spring with the most delicious water. This would turn out to be our little green valley.

Our folks intended to build a house in 1927, but thank heavens they didn't. A forest fire raged throughout the area that summer until it reached the edge of the tiny community. A railroad locomotive with a passenger coach was ordered to the town to pick up the women and children, and my mother along with my three oldest sisters were among those that went. Along the tracks fires were burning, and on several occasions the train had to be stopped in order that burning trees could be taken off the rails. When the train emerged from the smoke and fire, Mom said that the conductor threw his hat down and exclaimed, "Thank God we got these women and children out of there."

Back at the mill site my father and the others who stayed were making a last ditch effort to save the sawmill and the few homes that were there. They had constructed several rafts of logs with which they were prepared to push out into the river at the last moment. When the fire approached them with flames going hundreds of feet above the tree tops, all seemed lost. Then, in an instant, the wind changed and blew the fire back into itself and all the buildings were saved.

The next year my parents built their dream home in this burnt over valley and there it stands to this day.

My mom played the organ as well as the piano and my dad played the violin, so our home always had an abundance of music available. All through the years there were parties in our home with fun and laughter the order of the day. Both parents had a tremendous sense of humour, an attribute that I have always tried to sustain as I think it really makes life worth living.

My father worked at many different jobs throughout the years, but it was always his tales of adventures in the forests that captivated me. Both Mom and Dad worked so very hard throughout their lives and my dad liked to party hard as well. There are so many wonderful and funny memories I have of my dad and mom. I wouldn't trade them for all the treasures on earth.

When my brothers Joe, Clarence and I were quite young, I guess my dad figured that we were always going to be into something or other, so it would be good if he knew what it was. With that in mind, he called us boys together and told us that he had lost the thing-a-ma-jig off the grindstone. He then pulled a crisp new $5.00 bill out of his pocket and told us that it was the prize for whoever

Bessie and Joe Boudreau with daughters Isie and Evie in Penny, 1925.

found the missing part. Man! I did some quick calculating and realized just how many chocolate bars that would buy, and said I was in. All that summer I patrolled the fields and looked along the stream that meandered through our farm, but I was unable to find it. Trouble was, I didn't know what a thing-a-ma-jig looked like, so I wouldn't have known what it was if I found it. No matter, the thought of that $5.00 was all the impetus needed to keep me looking. A couple years passed before I finally realized that there never was a thing-a-ma-jig on the grindstone to start with.

This was a good description of the type of humour my dad possessed, and he always put it to good use.

One of my most priceless memories is of a Christmas party at our home. Among the guests was a big Norwegian named Ole. A kindhearted and lovable fellow, he and my dad used to tip a few now and then. Well, this night Ole tipped a few too many drinks and then took a shine to a lovely young thing who had some accessories he appeared to be interested in. He took after her and started following her around the house. We tried our best to distract him and when that didn't work, we decided to ply him with booze in the hope that he would go to sleep. That was mistake number one. Every time Ole turned around, someone would have another drink waiting for him and he would take a pull out of a bottle of whiskey like you can't imagine. After each one of these big pulls he would exclaim, "Yesus!" Well, we kept plying him with booze and after about an hour he laid down on our chesterfield and fell asleep. Trouble was he looked terribly uncomfortable as his neck was hanging over the edge. We felt sorry for him so we decided to move him into a more comfortable position. This was mistake number two.

Ole was a huge man and must have weighed almost 300 pounds, so we had a time moving him. All of a sudden he stood up and said, "What in Yesus is going on around here." Back into the party he went and started chasing the lovely young thing with the nice accessories around the house again. Well, by this time Dad had seen enough and decided to take Ole home. This was mistake number three. Dad harnessed our team of horses, hooked them up to the sleigh, and together we managed to get Ole aboard. And so they departed. The party carried on and about nine o'clock in the morning, someone said, "There comes Dad." We looked out the window, but it sure didn't look like Dad driving the team. When it came closer we suddenly realized that Ole was driving the team and Dad was nowhere to be seen. We rushed out the door and met Ole coming back into the party, and when he passed us he didn't offer any explanation, he just said, "Yesus!"

Several of us rushed out and looked into the sleigh, and there was Dad sleeping peacefully while a half-bottle of whiskey rolled around beside him. We later learned that when they had arrived at Ole's house, Ole had asked Dad in for a drink and he had complied. That was mistake number four. Dad was only about half the size of Ole, so in a couple of hours he had drunk my dad right under the table, so to speak. Once that was done, he loaded him in the sleigh like a sack of wheat and brought him back home, then rejoined the party.

Fortunately, the lovely young thing had departed.

After that, whenever someone started getting out of hand at one of our parties, one of us would say, "They'd better smarten up or we'll have to get Dad to take them home." Man! That bit of humour sure wore thin in a hurry.

Many of the funniest stories took place in Prince George after trapping season, and after the winter logging season was over, when woodsmen of all stripes would head into town to have a few drinks and meet people they otherwise would seldom see. My dad was no exception, and he just loved to hit the city a couple times a year to do a little partying. Understandably, some of the events that took place were quite hilarious.

On one trip to Prince George my dad had been staying at the Prince George Hotel for a few days when he got in touch with me and suggested we go out for lunch. We went to the Shasta Cafe where Dad surprised me by asking the waitress if he could have a bowl of mush (porridge). The waitress gave him a suspicious look and said, "Sir, it's afternoon!" Dad didn't give up, though, he persisted by saying that it sure would be nice. After giving Dad a very searching look, she said, "I'll ask the cook." A minute later she came back and affirmed that the cook said it was okay.

Suddenly, Dad almost jumped out of his chair, looked at his watch, and exclaimed, "It's after 2 o'clock! I forgot to pay for the hotel room for tonight!" I tried to assure him that it would be all right if he was a few minutes late with the money, but he came back with, "You can't trust those buggers, they might throw my suitcase out in the street. Let's go!" Since I wasn't in the mood for a bowl of mush, and since Dad was already heading for the door, I followed. With Dad in the lead we crossed the floor, and as we went out the door I glanced back to see the waitress standing at our table with the bowl of mush in her hand. I think it's safe to say that if looks could kill we both would have cashed in our chips that day. She gave us a withering look of contempt that still haunts me to this day. I also must add that I stayed away from that cafe for at least five years.

I recall another time Dad came to town and we went out for a few beer. In the pub we met two men who joined us at our table. One man was John Humphries, a shipper by trade, and the other was a fellow named Bud Ganton, a real comical fellow who did various jobs for a living. After we had a couple beers, someone suggested that a shot of whiskey would sure hit the spot. Dad said that we should come to his room at the National Hotel as he had a bottle there, so away we went. When we arrived at the hotel, Dad got out his key to open the door to his room, but it didn't want to yield. He kept at it, though, and eventually got it opened. As we entered I was shocked to see a woman sitting on the bed. Then several things happened at once. The lady on the bed smiled at Dad; Mr. Humphries looked at me and raised his eyebrows a considerable distance as much as to say, "Why the old bugger! Can you believe this?" Bud Ganton looked at me and winked; I gestured with my hands that I didn't know anything about this woman. And, at the same instant, I'm ashamed to admit, I had a mental image of Dad and this woman pounding the mattress. Well, Dad and this woman looked at each other for a minute, then Dad backed up and looked at the room number on the door. "Excuse me!" he said, then headed out the door and down the hallway to the next room which was his, while I tagged along, just a bit disgusted at how quick people are to jump to conclusions — myself among them.

This Bud Ganton fellow was always out for a laugh, and he got a chance for a good one when Dad went to a spring party at Bud's home in Prince George. They partied until all hours, and Dad finally fell asleep at the table. Bud helped him into a bedroom and put him to bed, then added some bras and panties. Next morning they were sitting in the kitchen, listening, when Dad woke up. They heard him talking French, something he hadn't done since he left New Brunswick as a teenager. When he came out of the bedroom, they asked what went on in there. He explained that after finding the bras and panties, he looked out the window and it reminded him of a place where he stayed in Quebec City 40 years earlier. The French he spoke translated into, "Good God! What's Momma gonna say now?"

My dad didn't just have a great sense of humour, he also had that split-second timing that is so necessary to pulling off a good joke. I'm thinking of one Saturday night in the Penny Community Hall when the place was rocking. Right in the middle of a dance tune with the band playing loudly, the electric generator that was the power source for the hall failed. In a few seconds, the hall was transformed to silent darkness. Instantly, echoing the thought that may have been in the minds of several of the men, my dad shouted in a very loud voice, "Where's my wife?" In a moment, the lights went up and there wasn't a person in the hall who wasn't rolling with laughter.

I think my favorite, though, was the story of the sledge hammer. This story started when Dad couldn't find his sledge hammer. He looked everywhere he could think of and after about one month just gave up. One day he was walking through the property of another Penny resident, when he saw his sledge hammer leaning against this man's shed. Well, Dad knew that this man had a reputation for having light fingers, which meant that when he walked by, things had a habit of jumping into his hands and leaving with him. Dad looked and no one seemed to be around, so he put the sledge hammer under his coat and brought it home where he informed us that he had "fixed that bugger." Just a couple of days later, Dad went up on the hill behind our house to work on the fence repair he had started the previous year and there on the ground was his sledge hammer. That night, under cover of darkness, my dad returned the other sledge hammer to the previous and perhaps rightful owner.

Humour is a tricky thing and it can easily backfire, as my dad found out one day. We were all sitting at the kitchen table after eating when the conversation turned to discussing women. Just for a joke, Dad winked at us and said, "Only the mother knows who the father is." Well, Mom didn't see the wink, so in less that a heartbeat she waved her finger right in front of Dad's nose and stated, "Now see here! You remember that party we had in the cookhouse about 30 years ago? Well, me and Mrs. Ells were the only ones left inside. The rest of you were out in the dark, drinking and carrying on and whatever!"

By the time Mom finished her statement, Dad had squirmed out of his chair, grabbed his hat, and was heading out the door. Apparently, something needed doing down at the blacksmith shop.

Humour was always in abundance for those who could see it, even during the First World War when men tried to evade the military draft. One such gentleman said that he used to spend every Thursday in the woods because that was when the police would come looking for him. There were also the draft evaders who stayed across the Fraser River from Longworth. These men shot a moose out of season and were reported by one of the townspeople. The game warden was sent out to do his duty and when he started across the river, a barrage of gunfire erupted from the other side. He quickly turned his boat around and returned to Prince George, his boat somewhat lighter because of all the bullet holes.

Another story tells of a policeman's visit to a farm to check for the man of the house who had not answered his call to duty. The lady of the house — who was unwell and therefore house-bound — assured the officer that she had not seen her husband in months. In his walk around the farm, the policeman — who himself had been raised on a farm — noticed something peculiar. The bags of the milk cows did not appear to be full of milk, in fact, they looked decidedly empty. That evening just as darkness fell, a shadow emerged from the forest with a milk pail in one hand and walked right into the arms of the waiting policeman.

Quite often these men would take the chance of getting caught by coming home occasionally, especially the married men. It appears obvious that the authorities were turning a blind eye to them. In some cases the men that were caught seemed to be treated lightly. Like Mr. Kline and Axel Anderson who were fined $10 and $15 respectively for military delinquency on September 18, 1918.

A story with a very human touch occurred in the McBride area when a Shere-area man reported his neighbour for shooting a moose out of season. The investigation fell to Constable McKinley, who quickly found the moose carcass. The perpetrator, who was only trying to feed a lot of hungry mouths, was hauled into court. When the magistrate informed him that the penalty was $15 or 30 says, the man replied, "Your Honour, I haven't seen $15 in years."

The magistrate then summoned Constable McKinley to approach the bench where they huddled in whispered conversation for a few minutes. Suddenly they both pulled out their wallets and each threw $7.50 on the bench. The conviction stood, but the man was allowed to go home.

Lloyd Jakeman, who was with the Prince George City Police Force, told me the following story: "We arrested a man for being intoxicated in a public place, as many were want to do. This chap was walking down the street taking pulls out of a whiskey bottle, so we took him to jail. While there, we asked him to clean up the office of the jail. This guy appeared to be a slow worker, though, because it took him almost the entire weekend to get the job done. Well, when court proceedings started, the accused and several others facing similar charges had to be released because someone had drunk up all the evidence."

The following story, taken from *The Citizen* of November 17, 1949, speaks for itself:

Logger Forgot to go to Jail

When Carl Anderson, a logger, appeared before Police Magistrate P. J. Moran on Thursday morning he had a lot of things to explain. Among these was the all important fact that he forgot to go to jail on September 17, when sentenced in the same court to serve 20 days on a charge of intoxication.

It seems that shortly after Carl received sentence, he was put to work by police on a woodpile, but an overpowering thirst seized him and guided his steps downtown to a local beer parlor. His courtroom explanation went like this:

ACCUSED: When I was in court I was still drunk and I forgot to come back.

MAGISTRATE: You were drunk in court?

ACCUSED: Not exactly drunk, just rum-dum Your Worship.

MAGISTRATE: Just rum-dum?

ACCUSED: When I went downtown I had one too many and a fellow offered me a job.

MAGISTRATE: That was six weeks ago and your memory failed you all that time?

ACCUSED: Yes, Your Worship.

MAGISTRATE: (after due deliberation) Twenty days in jail or $20 fine.

Accused is serving the 20 days.

≈≥

MANY LAUGHS WERE CREATED BY PEOPLE WHO TALKED TO themselves. Some people that spent many years alone would carry on such intense conversations with themselves that from a little distance, one would think there was a whole group of people.

One such man lived beside the railroad grade about seven miles west of Penny. Even in his 70s, he would walk the 14-mile round trip to Penny and back to get his mail and buy groceries. A retired woodsman, Dunc McLeod used to be a logger who was experienced at building ice roads, for the easy transportation of logs from the forest — a talent he carried on into retirement.

One winter day a man named Mr. Berginc decided to walk the three miles from Longworth to visit Dunc. When he arrived at the cabin it was deserted, but he noticed an ice road leading back into the forest, so he decided to follow it. After going just a short distance, he heard hollering further back in the forest and fearing that Dunc was injured, he hurried along as fast as he could until he reached a spot where he could see Dunc through the trees. He had built a harness for himself and was hooked up to a huge load of firewood. With

Mr. Berginc staring in amazement, Dunc would shout "pull" and then lunge ahead in a futile attempt to get the overloaded sleigh moving. Several times this sequence was repeated until at last he shouted in a very loud voice, "Are you going to pull or do I have to cut a switch?" Fearing that he may very well "cut a switch," Mr. Berginc went to him and together they managed to get the sleigh moving.

An elderly Prince George trapper named Harry Weaver told me the following story. It was supposed to have taken place in the '50s, but there was a twinkle in his eye when he told it, so I wouldn't bet on it being anything but a joke.

Apparently a trapper rushed into a Prince George jewelry store late on a Saturday afternoon and hollered, "Quick, I need a ring for my girl friend." The clerk pulled one out and placed it on the counter.

"How much?" asked the trapper.

"One hundred ninety dollars." replied the clerk.

"That's way too much," allowed the trapper.

"Well here's one for $75." countered the clerk.

"How come they're so expensive?"

"Well, they're diamond, and a diamond is forever."

Trapper, "Well, I was hoping you have something for around $5 or $10 that will last until tomorrow morning."

6

DOME CREEK

Now I would like to move 13 miles east of Penny along the CNR to the town of Dome Creek. During the heyday of trapping, Dome Creek was a busy outfitting center for trappers, guides, and prospectors. It served the upper McGregor and Herrick watersheds, as well as the Ptarmigan, Slim, and Dome Creek watersheds and the main Fraser River valley. This encompassed a huge geographic area.

Many well-known and colourful individuals made Dome Creek their base of operations at one time or another. An example was carried in the *Prince George Citizen* of May 23, 1921:

Real Old Westerner will Prospect District
Charlie Kendall, Once Pony Express Rider with Buffalo Bill, Strikes This District

After sixty-eight years of a life lived in the West and crammed full of color and romance, Charlie Kendall, one of the last of the old plains riders, got off the train at Prince George last week resolved to adopt this country for his prospecting field in future.

For many years Kendall washed gold on Gold Creek, a tributary of the Skeena river. He was the discoverer of the Toulon Mine, near Usk. This mine was later partly owned by the late Charles Clifford, the first member for Cassiar, who years ago put in a winter here at the Hudson's Bay Company's Post.

Believing that this country promises good territory for the experienced prospector, Kendall will range the hills, with Dome Creek as his headquarters, in the future. The country, he says, looks good to him, and he hopes that the hills will reveal to his wise and searching eye, some of the secrets of mineral wealth which they most certainly contain. In spite of his sixty-eight years Kendall is still as active and erect as men in their prime.

The history of this man would make very interesting reading. As a boy, in company with young Cody, who later gained world fame as Buffalo Bill, he became one of the United States' Pony Express Riders, developing subsequently into an Indian fighter and army scout. With the settlement of the West, Kendall took up land, and the site of the present city of Omaha was his first homestead.

New men and manners were too much for the spirit of the westerner, who, by easy stages, followed the path of the setting sun until he eventually reached British Columbia.

In 1914, when the clarion call for men went out through the west, Kendall quickly responded and he served for two years with the Canadian forces.

ANOTHER MAN WHO TRAPPED OUT OF DOME CREEK WAS John Ogilvie Skookum Davidson, a rancher, trapper and pack train operator who became a living legend in northern BC. Born in Scotland, he came to Canada at the age of 14 and travelled across the country to BC, where he first earned a living as a ranch hand and packer.

During the First World War he served overseas where he won several medals for bravery. After the war he returned to BC and ran pack-horse trains for government surveys, travelling all over the northern part of the province.

It was in the summer of 1932 that Skook arrived in Dome Creek where he decided to try his hand at trapping. Together with a friend named John Gaspery and his own ever present horses, they headed up across the McGregor River through what is now McCullagh Creek into the upper Herrick Creek; to the same trapline where Tom Meaney was killed by a huge boar grizzly six years earlier. They cut a winter's supply of firewood and stocked with food, the two main cabins that Skook would use the following winter. When the work had been completed they struck out for home only to find the valley socked in tight with cloud. A short time later they discovered why former trappers had named it Blunder Pass when they found themselves confused in two adjacent passes that looked and felt alike.

Skook then showed John his knowledge and trust of horses when he let one go and then followed it. In 20 minutes they were at the right exit and homeward bound.

Skook spent the winter of 1932/33 trapping the upper Herrick, a winter of heavy snowfall during which the fur wouldn't move, with the result that he just "ate up his grub."

It was as a young man that he first earned the name Skookum from the Chinook dialect meaning strong, and he got it by carrying 200-lb. packs on his back into his first ranch where everything had to be taken in by trail.

After travelling much of the province, Skook first visited the Kechika River Valley in 1939, and it was love at first sight. It was here that he built the Diamond J. Ranch and lived alone for many years about 100 miles south of Watson Lake. At times he ran as many as 200 horses, and his guiding rights covered over 5000 square miles.

In the early 1940s Arne Jensen helped Skook on a cattle drive when they took the first herd of cattle into the ranch and was struck by its beauty. Built somewhat like a grizzly himself, Arne agreed that Skook was a "powerful brute." Also in the 1940s Skook was given

Skook Davidson, (second from right), Arne Jensen (far right) at Skook's ranch. c. 1935.

the rank of Special Constable in the BC Police Force because his knowledge of the North was extremely valuable in remote areas.

Any story of trapping and guiding in Dome Creek would be incomplete without mentioning Jim Hooker. Jim came to Dome Creek with his wife in 1913 during construction of the Grand Trunk Pacific Railroad. For a short while they stayed in a railway boxcar while Jim built a log cabin into which they moved that November. As the cabin had been hastily constructed out of green logs, they spent a miserable winter enduring the seemingly endless moisture that emanated from the green logs. Because it had been a late fall Jim had managed to get up enough hay in November to winter their cow and so with their first winter under their belt, they were well on their way.

Jim's first run-in with a moose was an experience he wouldn't soon forget. He wounded the beast and chased it for miles before getting it. He quickly learned that the .22 high power he possessed was okay for deer in Indiana, but was not adequate for big game in BC. Despite this, Jim became a well-known trapper and guide who always produced game for his hunters. For many years he guided and trapped the Torpy River area. In one fall in the late '30s, Jim took in $3600 from fall guiding alone, a considerable sum of money at that time.

When I was just a young lad I remember Jim coming to visit my dad, and I certainly recall the time he told Dad that moose lost their antlers because they froze off. He had noticed that if the temperature dropped to -30°F or colder in November, for instance, that the moose had dropped their antlers by Christmas. Alternately he had also noticed that if it was a warm winter, the moose would carry them into late winter.

Jim's sons told me a story about a man known as Red Martin, a fellow who reportedly made a habit out of poaching on other people's traplines. It seems that Jim was leaving his line one spring day when he stopped at the Slide cabin and noticed smoke coming from the stovepipe. He hollered, "Who's there?"

"Don't shoot, Jim, it's me," came the reply as Red came out of the cabin. He had an abundance of traps with him and was no doubt intent on doing a bit of beaver trapping on Jim's line. Jim invited him back into the cabin where he made a big meal for him, then asked him to promise that he would never come on his trapline again. Once he received the promise, Jim took Red across the Torpy River in his riverboat, dropped him off on the opposite bank, and said, "I'm keeping your traps, Red, and you can walk out from here." Red pleaded for a ride back out, saying that it was a long walk. Jim responded that it was exactly the same distance out as it had been for him to walk in. Red walked.

Jim's son, Lawrence Hooker, had an experience with Red while he was sharing a trapline with Shorty Haynes near Pass Lake. Shorty was out at the time when Lawrence packed in to the cabin, only to find Red there. He was out of food and, more importantly, out of pipe tobacco. Lawrence suggested they walk over onto Jim's line and pick up some caribou meat that was there. Red refused to go and when questioned said, "I promised Jim that I would never set foot on his line again, and I meant it." Lawrence insisted it would be okay as long as he was with him, so they went. When they arrived at Jim's cabin, they were in for a pleasant surprise: someone had left some pipe tobacco in the cabin and Red took full advantage of it. Lawrence said that he never saw anyone so contented in all his life.

Red Martin seemed to have a penchant for getting caught poaching. After one episode of a similar nature, he went into Prince George and proceeded to go on a binge which lasted for several days. He then went and purchased a new Stetson, walked down to the Fraser River and put the Stetson on the bank. Then, for his final act, he filled his pockets with rocks and jumped in.

In all fairness to these so-called poachers, we must remember that prior to the registration of traplines on crown land, it was open season, or first-come, first-serve, obviously leading people to understand that the fur belonged to everyone. This new legislation took some time to sink in. Often two different trappers would find they had company on their lines, a situation that could and did lead to serious problems. Others looked at it more philosophically, like Ernest Jensen and another trapper, who were both trapping the same line at one time. Someone asked Ernest why he allowed that person to trap on what some considered was Ernest's line. Ernest responded in his Danish accent, "Jesus Cwyst, the man's got a family."

Before we leave the early days of the Dome Creek area, it is a must to mention an event that drew considerable interest there. It occurred up Slim Creek, about 10 miles south west of Dome Creek and was carried in the February 27, 1920 edition of the *Prince George Citizen:* "...Two of the members of Mr. Burden's party, George Broderick and Allan Henderson, were working on the cutting of a new trail to the party's next camp. They had a puppy with them which ran about in the business-like way that puppies do, while the men were working. It appears that the little dog ran upon a moose, which chased it through the woods until pup and moose arrived suddenly upon Broderick and Allan working on their trail. The infuriated moose charged Broderick, who, taken by surprise, jumped and broke his snowshoe, leaving him at the mercy of the animal. The moose struck him a cruel blow on the shoulder with a front hoof and would undoubtedly have killed him had it not been for Allan's quick work with the axe. He struck the moose on the head, breaking its skull, and finished it off with a few blows." Broderick, who was chief cruiser for Upper Fraser Lumber Co. of Dome Creek, was unable to return to work for some time.

There were many dangers facing these woodsmen, and not all were posed by animals. Jim Hooker's son Ken describes a near date with disaster in the early '60s when he and a friend named Hubert Cropley headed up the Fraser for the Torpy River: "It was late fall and the ice was running heavy in the Fraser, but we thought we could get through to the Torpy River. We managed to get upriver as far as Mile 50, which is where the river and the railroad run side by side. Then we got stuck in the ice and right away the ice jammed and stopped, so we were stuck. I tried to get the outboard motor off the back of the boat so it wouldn't freeze in the ice but in the process, I fell in the river. Once I got back in the riverboat, I poured some of the gasoline in a metal pail and lit a fire in an attempt to keep warm. We tried to walk on the heavy slush, but it wouldn't support us so we were trapped. Our only hope was that a train would pass and they would see us and send help. Well, we were there for several hours and really getting cold when a train came by, but we fired our rifles and thank God, they heard the shots. The crew of the train then notified the BC Forest Service at Penny, who came up and placed planks on the ice. By the time they got out to our boat, we were burning the last of the gasoline."

Ken had another day to remember with his brother Lawrence, in 1971. Lawrence had returned from California to the area he had grown up in, the same area where he had spent 53 days trapping as a lad of 15 without seeing another person. Now he had come back, hoping to get a grizzly bear.

This is the story as Ken related it to me: "Lawrence came up from California to see if he could get a grizzly, so we headed up the Torpy River for a spring hunt in my guiding territory. We left Dome Creek and made it up to the Slide Cabin where we intended to spend the night. A short time after we got there, I went outside to use the outdoor biffy. While I was sitting there, I heard something approaching and opened the door to find a black bear heading toward me. I thought I would just scare it away, so I shouted, 'What are you doing here?' Instead of running away, though, it came straight at me, so I slammed the door and hooked it. This only made the bear more determined and it immediately began tearing lumber off the door. I really got worried then, so I hollered as loud as I could, trying to get Lawrence's attention. I also did my best to discourage the bear by kicking it, but this only inspired it to greater effort. At one point, the bear left the door area and went around the side of the biffy, where it began tearing boards off the wall. There was a tin can in the toilet, so I put it over my fist and slugged the bear on the nose just as hard as I could, but it didn't even fizz on it. It just paid no attention."

"Were you concerned for your life?" I asked.

"You're darned right I was. I found out just how helpless a man is against an animal like that, and it wasn't even a big bear. Anyway, I was yelling as loud as I could and Lawrence and his wife, Lee, heard the commotion but because of the noise from the creek that ran under the cabin, they didn't know what it was. They thought it was a flock of geese on the river. Finally, Lawrence came out for a look and could hardly believe his eyes. He ran back into the cabin and came out with his rifle, but I yelled at him not to shoot, because the bear was right between us, and I thought he might hit me. Then Lawrence called to it and right away it ran toward him, so he shot it."

"He probably saved you from being the guest of honor at a spring banquet," I commented.

"No doubt. You know that poor animal was starving; it was really thin. We saw where its tracks came down the mountainside. I'm sure it heard us and in its old starving condition, it immediately attacked. If I had been alone that day he most certainly would have killed and eaten me, I couldn't believe how helpless I was."

Ken's brother, Glen Hooker, who also guided out of Dome Creek, had his own mix-up with a bear when he guided two Pennsylvania hunters up Ptarmigan Creek. "They were after grizzly bears," Glen started, "and we finally managed to spot one on a mountain about a quarter-mile away. The bear had sensed our presence and was moving away up the mountain when the two hunters took a chance and fired. I wanted them to wait, because that bear was about 400 yards away. Anyway, they fired and one of them managed to hit the bear which then ran away into the trees. One hunter circled to get above the spot where it had last been seen, while I followed the other hunter right to the spot. We were following the blood trail when suddenly the bear jumped out of a thicket right on top of that hunter. The bear grabbed the hunter by the upper arm and together they went rolling end over end down the mountainside, while I ran behind them, shouting to the hunter, 'Drop your gun! Drop your gun!'"

Lawrence and Ken Hooker with bear that came for lunch, 1971.

"You mean he was still holding his rifle?" I asked.

"No! The strap of the rifle was wrapped around his arm above the spot where the bear had hold, so he was unable to drop it. After a minute, the bear let go of the hunter's arm to get a new grip, and this gave me the chance to grab the gun and finish it off."

"How serious were his wounds?" I asked.

"His injuries were not too bad, not bad enough to have to take him out to the hospital. Between me and my wife Myra, we were able to patch him up enough so that he could finish the hunt."

Another Dome Creek resident who tangled with a grizzly was not quite so fortunate. His name was Heller Hreczka. In 1963 I listened to the story of his adventure and noticed the many battle scars he still carried from the one-sided encounter. "This happened on the night of October 21, 1961," Heller began. "I was walking the railway tracks from Dome Creek back to Bend, which lies a couple miles to the

Glen Hooker at up-river cabin, 1948.

west. It was about 11 o'clock when it happened. As I neared Bend where I worked as a section hand, I heard something moving rapidly toward me. There was a bit of moonlight and it gave me enough light to see the way but when I heard the noise, I pulled my flashlight from my pocket and turned it on. Then I saw a grizzly barreling right into me. It struck me a blow across my face and as I was falling, it hit me a glancing blow across my arm. Then in an instant, it was gone. When I went to protect my face, I had put my hand up and the bear bit it and severed the tendons in my finger and you can see it's all twisted."

"Did it knock you unconscious?" I asked.

"No! But I knew I was hurt bad. Well, I managed to make it back to Bend and the section foreman couldn't believe it when he seen me. I was all covered with blood and I still had a handful of the bear's hair that I had grabbed without realizing it. I was in a state of shock, but he bandaged me up as good as he could and then stopped a freight train which took me to McBride Hospital."

"What was the final damage report?" I asked.

"Well, the blow to my face had broken my jaw, fractured my cheekbone, and laid me open for 30 stitches; the blow that creased my arm, laid me open for an additional 20. It was a full year before I completely recovered from my wounds, and I'm telling you that for a year or two after that, any unusual noise in the woods would make my hair stand on end."

The day following his mauling, a party returned to the scene and attempted to piece together the events of the evening before. About one week earlier a domestic cow had been killed by a train and the section crew had buried it there, not realizing that it takes more than a foot of earth to cheat a bear's keen sense of smell. A grizzly and cub had found it and at the moment Heller happened along, the sow was feeding on it and the cub was on the other side of the railway tracks. Heller felt that the bear did not sense his presence until he was right between them, a perilous situation even for an armed man.

Before I leave the Dome Creek country, I would like to lighten things up with a humorous story that simply must be told. I have been told that it was the going joke all around the area just prior to

1920. It concerns a bachelor known as James Scotty Stewart who owned a store in the tiny community of Snowshoe, several miles to the east of Dome Creek. One day a local resident burst into the store and asked Scotty if he would assist a woman that was about to give birth because there was no one else around to help. Agreeing that he would try to assist, he threw in a timeless bachelor complaint by saying, "Sure, they call for me when they're calving, but they sure never call for me when they're bulling."

7

REGULATIONS

I HAVE HAD PEOPLE TELL ME THAT THEY SIMPLY COULD NOT have made it without the extra money that came in from furs. And that even with it, they went through perilous times. Since trapping was such an important part of people's lives, I want to include a very brief summary of some of the legislation that came down and the reasons for it.

Trapping regulations were enacted in BC in 1906, to aid in management. During the early years of trapping, there were many horror stories of traplines being raped by trappers who would then simply move on to a new location where they could do the same thing again. Nowhere did this become more apparent than in the trapping of beaver, which were pushed to the point of extinction. This led to a regulation prohibiting the trapping of beaver in 1919, which was quickly followed by a great deal of protesting by trappers who felt they were losing a very necessary part of their incomes. The protests were in turn followed by a very heated response from Dr. A. R. Baker, Chairman of the BC Conservation Board:

"The fur dealers and trappers were not satisfied with legitimate methods and were heading toward a quick extermination of beaver in BC. All the protests they can make will not remove the closed season. The killing of beaver is closed and will stay closed until the board opens it again." Mr. Baker then went on to say, "Anyone found with any portion of a green beaver pelt would be prosecuted and that the burden of proof lay on the person possessing same."

It was also in 1919 that the fur industry in the Interior really came to the fore with reports that nearly $500,000 worth of fur had been sold from the district lying between Hazelton and Lucerne (just west of the Alberta border) with Prince George shipments alone totaling $200,000.

Fur shipments from Prince George during the 1917/18 season included: beaver 5584, rats 4005, red fox 175, cross fox 192, silver fox 62, mink 783, skunk 58, bear 100, lynx 1621, fisher 579, coyotes 420, ermine 4914, otter 115, marten 1588 and wolverine 38.

After many charges of unethical dealings by fur traders, fur trader licences were enacted in April 1920. These traders sometimes got stung by manufacturers who entered the market paying more than quoted prices for a desired line of fur. This, in turn, would lead to rumours and speculation which was not realized by many disillusioned trappers. Proof that the traders were not immune was shown when fur trader Ivor Guest sold his 1921 season's buy of muskrats in Montreal for $1.00 each, the same price he had paid for them in the North. At this same time another Prince George trader, Ernest Livingstone, was in Detroit, trying to regain his $1.00 per pelt for muskrats. His highest offer in New York had been 80 cents.

A classic example of a fur trader getting stung occurred when a greenhorn trader arrived in Prince George. It wasn't long before he purchased a bob-tailed coyote from a wily old trapper. When he went to market he saw it auctioned off as a lynx, which was worth far less money at the time. Apparently this same trader bought several small beaver pelts and then was surprised to see them go as muskrats, which again were worth less.

Probably the best piece of trapping legislation ever passed occurred in 1926 and was the registration of traplines on crown land. During the last two weeks of May about 400 applications were dealt with in the Prince George Game Office. *The Citizen* dated April 1, 1926, stated: "...in the registration of traplines both trappers and game officials are agreed there will come an improvement in the supply of fur-bearers, in that the owners of the traplines are given an incentive to husband the game supplies in their respective territories and the chance to build up their traplines so that they may have a good selling value in the event of their deciding to retire from the business."

It was a slow procedure getting laws with teeth. Often law-breakers got off with little more than a slap on the wrist — like the Hazelton man who got off with a $20 fine for possession of 70 beaver pelts.

Steady pressure was brought to bear by the BC Registered Trappers' Association in cases of fur theft. In one instance President Eric Collier of Riske Creek made the comparison that the theft of a single fur from a city warehouse might bring a sentence of two years, whereas a fine of $10 was sometimes imposed for theft of a fur from a trapline.

On July 12, 1936, the Hudson's Bay Post at Fort Nelson was robbed of $32,000 worth of fur. Pilot Ginger Coote flew out of Prince George with Provincial Constables Frank Cook and William Forrester on a search and investigation that led them around the forests for almost a whole month. Because the aircraft was fixed with floats and the spots where it could land were widely separated, the constables had to cover long distances on foot, carry their supplies on their backs, and sleep wherever night caught them. In one trek Constable Cook covered a distance of 125 miles in a three and one-half day walk through the forest.

Eventually two men Bert Sheffield and Harry Labourcay were arrested and charged. After lengthy court proceedings they were found guilty in October 1937 and sentenced to five years in the pen.

Trapping without a licence appeared to be taken very seriously, as evidenced by a Mr. Whitberg of Finlay Forks who was convicted of same in 1919 and sentenced to a $250 fine or four months in jail. He chose jail.

In later years, trappers and hunters managed to augment their incomes somewhat by bounty hunting. Cougar, the tracks of which were first seen in the Prince George area about 1919, were worth $15, while wolves were $10, and the bounty on coyotes was $5. These prices were raised a few years later.

This bounty hunting of wolves was a hit-and-miss business and more often than not, it was a complete miss, as attested to by the following story.

Trapper Harry Weaver of Prince George told me of one trip that he, his brother Fleet, Bob McMillan, and Lawrence Hooker of Dome Creek, took after wolves: "It was during the winter of 1939/40 that we decided to make our fortunes as bounty hunters. We concentrated on an area between the Torpy and McGregor Rivers, and it was not long before we picked up the trail of a pack of 16. For 14 days we followed the pack, ending up on a ridge about 2000 feet above the main valleys. It was at this point that the wolf pack said, 'It's been fun — but...' The pack headed down over a very steep mountain-side, through the most impenetrable jungle imaginable, and then us four weary hunters returned home." Harry gathered his thoughts and then added, "Lawrence and Glen did persist, though, and managed to get six wolves a little later."

Often, the wolves that were taken resulted from someone stumbling into a pack, or in other words, were the result of luck not skill. Some bounty hunters got skunked and gave up; others were more successful, or luckier.

One of the most successful wolf hunters was a farmer, trapper, and hunter named Joe Lavoie of Batnuni Lake. During the winter of 1941, he accounted for 13 wolves and 15 coyotes. He claimed that the wolf packs were large and the animals weighed over 150 pounds each. On

Harry Weaver with unusual moose foot from moose he shot in 1936.

one hunt he ran into a large pack and got eight animals. He also claimed that the deer and his own calves were continuous victims.

The war against wolves became even more apparent as evidenced by this *Prince George Citizen* article dated June 8, 1950:

200 Wolves Less in Four Months

If there is a considerable increase in game this year and henceforth it will be largely due to the efforts of the Game Department's two predatory hunters, Dan Nennison and H. J. Harrison, who, during the four months from January to April, poisoned, trapped and snared almost 170 wolves.

In addition to the large number killed by the professional hunters, an additional 25 to 30 of the predatory beasts bit the dust as the result of private hunters' efforts.

It was during the winter of 1952/53, that the Game Branch really got serious about dealing with the wolf packs. *The Citizen* of 30 March 1953, carried this item:

Game Branch Completes
Huge Predator Poisoning Program
Over 30,000 Pounds of Bait Dropped

Probably more than 1000 wolves will have died in Northern BC by the time breakup comes as the result of the largest scale predator poisoning campaign ever carried out here.

BC Game Branch officials stationed in Prince George have put out close to 300 poisoned wolf baits using an estimated 34,000 pounds of horse meat.

Although of benefit to all hunters, guides and trappers, as well as being a strong deterrent to the spread of rabies, the program was financed by the Department of Indian Affairs for the protection of the livelihood of their native wards.

Approximately $2,000 was spent with Central BC Airways for flying time so that hundreds of isolated wolf concentrations could be reached.

The exact destructive force of the predator poisoning campaign will never be known in the form of number of wolves killed, but already trappers are reporting a sharp reduction in the number of ravenous packs.

One BC Game Branch bounty hunter operating his own aircraft to the west of Prince George has accounted for more than 50 wolves himself this winter, to say nothing of 45 coyotes.

Baits throughout the Prince George Game Division have been distributed as far north as Fort Ware to the north, Canoe Creek near Valemount to the east, the Blackwater River to the south and the Driftwood River to the west ...

ABOUT THIS TIME, THERE WERE NUMEROUS STORIES OF decimated wolf packs, and pack order that was completely destroyed. For the next few years there were many tales of wolves eating their own cubs or the weakest members of the pack because of starvation. The one I have picked as my favorite was told to me by a man named John Patrick, who was employed as a section foreman for many years by C N Railways. During a winter in the early '50s, he was patrolling the railroad with a three-man crew when they reached the end of their section. They took their motor car off the tracks on a take-off constructed for that purpose and waited for a freight train to pass before heading east again. As they sat silently in wait, their attention was drawn to some noise up on the hills above them. Suddenly they noticed four wolves making their way down the hill with great difficulty through the deep, loose snow. Unaware of their presence, three wolves attacked the smallest member of the pack and began tearing it apart. Feeling sorry for the wolf that was yelping in fright and pain, the men began hollering as loud as they could and were successful in distracting the three wolves. They immediately broke off their attack and headed down across the railroad grade toward the Fraser River. The injured wolf lay motionless in the snow for about 20 minutes, then dragged itself along the trail made by the other wolves until it apparently caught up with them. Although the men could not see them, they heard the yelping start up again for a short time and felt certain that the injured wolf had been killed.

All through the years, a debate has raged about whether wolves have killed a human being, or not. In my short search, I had no difficulty in finding a reported fatality. It is from the Prince George newspaper *The Leader,* dated April 2, 1922:

Killed by Timber Wolves

The body of Ben Cochrane, a trapper, was found torn to shreds north of Fisher River on Lake Winnipeg last week, having been attacked by a pack of timber wolves. His bones and pieces of his clothing and a rifle with a broken stock were found near.

Before succumbing to the pack, Cochrane shot seven wolves dead and clubbed four to death, their bodies lying around his tattered remains being the only evidence of his fight for life.

8

GRIZZLY ATTACK

IN 1968 I VISITED THE HOME OF JACK YARZEAU WHO LIVED in South Fort George. Jack was a trapper in his younger days and had been present when a close friend was attacked by a grizzly bear. This incident took place in the upper Herrick River, a tributary of the McGregor River. Jack began his story, "Because of the inherent danger of getting a serious injury, which often meant a certain and sometimes lingering death in the wilderness, many of us trappers developed a buddy system. Some of us shared a main cabin and then each ran their separate lines, returning to the main cabin at a pre-arranged date. This led to much peace of mind, because the sick or injured person know that help would be forthcoming. This arrangement also helped to ward off loneliness, one of our worst enemies out there in the forests. Well, it was for these reasons that Martin Deafy [pronounced Dee-fee] Dayton, Tom Meaney and I shared a main cabin in the upper McGregor River area during the '20s.

"Deafy was a local trapper," Jack went on, "but Tom had just came into the area a couple years earlier from the Barkerville area where he had trapped and guided with Frank Kibbee, a well-known man in that area.

"Tom told us about an encounter that Mr. Kibbee had experienced with a grizzly when he returned to a moose he had shot a few days earlier. Carrying only a axe, he walked right into a grizzly bear that was feeding on the carcass. Apparently the bear mauled Kibbee, and then left the scene. When Tom found him, he helped him out to medical attention and Mr. Kibbee completely recovered.

"Many times while we were sitting around the cabin in the evenings, Tom would retell this story, and we never tired of hearing it." Jack continued, "Then, on the morning of March 24, 1926, Tom left our Herrick Creek camp where we were tent-camping and went to get some meat off a moose that we had shot a few days before.

When he never returned to the tent that night I felt sure that something was terribly wrong, so I gathered some things together and got ready to search for him as soon as it got daylight.

"The way I remember it, I didn't get a wink of sleep that night. I knew that Tom had not bothered to take his rifle along and this really bothered me, as we all knew that boar grizzlies were up and about almost all winter."

"Did you think a bear was involved?" I asked.

"Well! not for certain. A lot of things could have happened, he could have fallen down and injured himself." Jack responded. "Anyway, as soon as it got daylight I left the cabin and followed Tom's tracks in the snow. About 20 minutes later, I walked onto a scene that I will never forget...."

The story was carried in the *Prince George Citizen* April 1, 1926:

Tom Meaney Killed by Grizzly Bear on McGregor River

Victim Was Engaged in Trapping
Along North Fork With Messrs. Yarzeau and Dayton

Was Surprised by a Bear and Forced
to Defend Himself With a Small Axe

Tom Meaney, who was engaged in trapping during the winter on the north fork of the McGregor River, was killed by a grizzly bear on Wednesday of last week, within one-half mile of his camp. Word of the fatality was brought to the city on Saturday by Jack Yarzeau, who was trapping in partnership with Meaney.

In the statement which Yarzeau made to the police he stated Meaney had left the camp on Wednesday morning to look over some traps and to attend to the cutting up of the carcass of a moose which had been killed some time before. Meaney was travelling on snowshoes and carried an axe but no rifle. As he did not return at night as had been expected, Yarzeau started out to look for him at 5 o'clock on Thursday morning. A short distance from the camp he came to the point where Meaney had discarded his snowshoes and continued his way on the crust of the snow.

The tracks led in the direction of the moose carcass and within half an hour Yarzeau came within sight of it. A short distance from the moose the body of Meaney was found. The face and top of the

head had been torn off and the brain was exposed. All around were
tracks of a grizzly bear. Meaney had been dead some time, and the
dead hand had a firm grip upon the handle of the axe.

Yarzeau says he immediately reported the death of Meaney to
Martin Dayton who undertook to look after it and try and get the
bear which killed him. He then made his way out to report the
death to the police.

Provincial Constable Muirhead has been sent out to the scene
of the tragedy, and the official account will not be available until
his return.

This *Citizen* article was followed by another dated April 15, 1926:

Record of Meaney's Fight with Silvertip Found in Snow

Trapper Made Gallant Defense With His Axe Until Bear Tore Away His Face

Big Game Hunters Should Get the Monster When Season Opens This Fall

Provincial Constable Muirhead returned to the city on Saturday
following a two-week trip into the Herrick River district to investigate the circumstances connected with the death of Thomas
Meaney, the trapper who was reported to have been killed by a
silvertip on Wednesday, March 24. The scene of the fatality was
on the Herrick River, about seventy miles from its confluence
with the McGregor. Dome Creek is used by the trappers in this
section as their outfitting point, and it means a trip of 100 miles.
The distance was covered by Constable Muirhead and Jack
Yarzeau in five days. The north wind was blowing and the nights
were bitter cold. On the mountains there are from eight to nine
feet of snow and in the valleys there are three and four feet.

There were no witnesses to the duel which Meaney fought
with the huge silvertip, but the record of the fight was left in the
clearest manner in the snow. Meaney left the tent camp which he
and Jack Yarzeau occupied at five o'clock in the morning of
March 24th. His mission was to look over some traps in the vicinity, some of which were close to a moose carcass which was being
used for food and bait. Not returning, Yarzeau started out to look
for him on the following morning, and came upon his mutilated
body not far from the moose carcass.

From the tracks left upon the snow the police officer had little difficulty in piecing together the story of the tragedy. The bear, which was an unusually large silvertip, had approached the carcass from a direction opposite to that taken by Meaney, the tracks of its hind feet measuring 14 inches long by 8 inches wide. The snow record showed that Meaney had got within 70 feet of the moose carcass when he gave battle with a three-pound axe. The bear had evidently seen Meaney before he saw the bear, and came on the run from the carcass in Meaney's direction. Within three or four feet from the point where Meaney had taken his last stand the bear reared up on his hind legs and commenced the fight. Within a circle of eighteen inches the snow was firmly tramped by Meaney, as he attempted to fight the bear off with the axe. There was but one imprint which showed the trapper had been forced out of his little circle and this was probably made when the bear landed the blow which knocked him over and killed him. This blow landed on the bridge of the nose, tearing it and the upper jaw away. From the markings in the snow the bear then jumped upon the body, pressing it deeply in the snow. With another stroke of one of its forepaws it tore off the front of the skull, and another blow ripped away the scalp from the rear of the head. The tracks indicated that the bear had run off after thus mutilating the body. In addition to these injuries it was found that Meaney's right hand had been cut by the bear, his left arm had been broken and there were several bruises on the chest and abdomen.

That the huge silvertip was hungry was evidenced by the fact that between the time of the encounter with Meaney and the arrival of the police officer it had made two attempts at returning to the carcass of the moose, but with the fear of wild animals for human remains, had retreated before coming up to them.

Thomas Meaney, the victim of the uneven duel, was not very well known in this section, coming in about nine months ago from the Barkerville section where he was formerly engaged as a big game guide with F. Kibbee. The axe used by Meaney in his fight with the bear was found a short distance from the body. It was blood-stained and there were a number of short hairs attached to it, and in the difference in the tracks made by the bear, it is thought Meaney severed three of the claws from the bear's left front foot.

THERE IS A DISCREPANCY IN THE POLICE REPORT AND THE
story as told to me by Jack Yarzeau. Jack, who was at the scene twice,
told me that the bear had definitely been injured by Tom's axe, but
that the spray of blood on the snow and willows, indicated an injury
higher on the body. The axe was still in the dead man's hand as indicated in the first report.

Understandably, these trappers did not relish the thought of a man-
killing grizzly travelling their traplines so they made an all-out effort
to get him. Deadfalls were set, bear traps were set and the men hunt-
ed it as well. Just which method was successful remains a contentious
issue with some people, but the following February, Deafy managed
to bag it and all the trappers in the area breathed a sigh of relief. The
following story was carried in *The Citizen* dated May 24, 1927:

Grizzly Which Killed Meaney is Shot by Trappers

Skull of the Animal Carries Mark of Wound on Jaw from Meaney's Axe
Deafy Dayton and Jack Yarzeau Got Bruin on Headwaters of the McGregor

Deafy Dayton arrived in the city this week with the skin and skull
of the bear which he asserts killed Thomas Meaney one year ago
today in a fight at the headwaters of the McGregor river. The skin
of the grizzly measures 9 by 5 1/2 feet, and Dayton is endeavor-
ing to dispose of it. He has had one offer of $60, but it is such a
fine specimen that he is holding out for $75.

The bear was taken by Dayton and his partner Jack Yarzeau,
who have been on the lookout for him since the killing of Meaney
and the skull was brought in to establish the fact that it is the bear
they were after. The lower jaw of the bear carries the evidence of
a very serious wound, there being evidence of a distinct fracture
running well into the jaw, which removed one tooth and drove
another fully half an inch out of alignment with the other teeth.
Dayton says it is plain the wound on the jaw was inflicted by a
severe blow with a sharp instrument such as an axe, the bone of
the jaw being cut very deep...

...Provincial Constable C. D. Muirhead visited the scene when
the killing had been reported and secured a number of interesting

photographs, through which it was possible to trace the various stages in the combat.

WHEN I VISITED JACK YARZEAU AT HIS HOME IN SOUTH FORT George in 1968, I asked him which method had been successful in taking the grizzly and he told me that Deafy had followed its tracks in the snow, caught up with it, and shot it.

The story of Meaney's fight with the grizzly was carried in almost every newspaper in the Dominion, and the following May, Meaney's brother in St. Agatha, Quebec, contacted Sergeant Walker of the provincial police in Prince George seeking to confirm that the dead man was his kin. A photograph was included which was shown to

Martin 'Deafy' Dayton with the skin of the grizzly that killed Tom Meaney.

Deafy Dayton, who assured the police that they were one and the same person.

During Constable Muirhead's trip into the Herrick Creek area to investigate the Meaney incident, he checked out the claim by Dayton that his dogs had just experienced a running battle with a pack of 20 wolves. Deafy showed the constable the abundant sign on the snow and convinced him that the story was true. It happened along the McGregor River when Deafy entered a patch of timber between two muskegs with his three dogs. As they moved through the timber, he noticed his dogs becoming very excited. Then they noticed the band of timber wolves about a quarter mile away. The dogs immediately took after the wolves, and Dayton watched the proceedings with interest. When the dogs got close, they seemed to change their minds and reversed direction, then it was the 20 wolves that were doing the chasing. As the three dogs came tearing back to him, Dayton fired and brought down one of the pack. This caused the others to turn tail and the show was over.

Martin Deafy Dayton certainly had a penchant for getting his name in the media. This appears to have started when he was 28 years of age when he wrote the following letter which was picked up and carried by the *Fort George Herald* dated November 27, 1915:

Some Reputation

There are a lot of bachelors in British Columbia who remain bachelors only because they "hant got the nerve to put a ad in a Paper to get a wafe" F. M. Dayton, obviously made of bolder stuff than the others, lets this fact be known in this letter received by The New York Times:

> Kidd, BC Mile 115, Oct. 22, 15
> The New York Times:
>
> Dear Sirs:
>
> I am writing this few lines in asking you has a Favor to Put this ad in your Paper. You see there is a lot of Batchlers out here and hant got the nerve to put a ad in a Paper to get a Wafe. has I am a Batch myself and looking for a Wafe and also I wood like to have you let it Run for about 3 ore 4 Days, and this is the ad.

WANTED A WAFE.

I am a Homesteader got 193 arcer of land. Dont Drink and a good
Worker. I am 28 years old. Wood like to hear from a girl from 18
to 28 years old. My address is, F. M. Dayton, Kidd, B. C., Mile
145 care of McBride Your truley, F. M. Dayton P. S. find inclose
1.00 Dollers if not a nuff let me know and will send Balense.

*Along with the other information that persons to whom the idea of
becoming a British Columbia "Wafe" appeals can find in the encyclopedia
are the facts that British Columbia is popularly called "A sea of mountains" and that the climate is somewhat warmer than the North Pole.*

DEAFY CARRIED ON WITH HIS LOVE AFFAIR WITH THE MEDIA,
and though his appeal for a "wafe" didn't bear fruit, I have been given
it on good authority that his love life never suffered because of it.

Throughout the last half of the 1920s, Deafy was the driving force
behind the annual trappers' dances in Prince George. At times his
outgoing personality struck a sharp contrast to the solitary life of a
trapper. *The Citizen* noted: "Martin Deafy Dayton was again the leading spirit in connection with the dance. He came in from Dome
Creek on Sunday evening and spent three days and three nights in
making preparations for the dance, and in getting out invitations to
all the trappers' friends to come and enjoy their hospitality for the
fourth time. The manner in which the hall was decorated instantly
broke down anything in the manner of formality. The company was
present as the guests of the trappers and they were welcomed under
surroundings typical of the trappers' life on the trapline. In the center of the dance floor was a large campfire, the necessary illusion
being furnished by the use of electric globes and red tissue paper, and
making an ideal setting. At different parts of the hall there were two
trappers' camps, arranged in realistic manner, and the entire hall was
given the semblance of the forest with the plentiful use of Jack pine
and spruce trees…"

These dances were so well organized and the guests made to feel
so welcome, that the hall was jammed to the point that "…To

attempt to dance during the evening was like taking part in a traffic block in one of the big cities."

An amusing incident took place at one of these trappers' dances when a trapper was assigned to door duty. Contrary to their open door policy, he decided there would be no gate-crashing. Shortly afterwards, the Provincial Police Sergeant Service decided to size up the party in preparation for some distinguished guests that were to arrive. The man at the door did not know the big sergeant and ordered him to leave, which the good-natured sergeant did. A short time later, Premier Tolmie, along with Lieutenant Governor Bruce arrived at the hall, whereupon the police sergeant flashed his badge to make sure that His Honor wasn't tossed out on his head. This done, the distinguished visitors were accorded a hearty welcome.

In 1937 Deafy shocked the other trappers in the region by bring-ing in the unheard-of catch of 44 coyote pelts which he got in the headwaters of the McGregor River. He expressed the belief that this was a real migration from the Prairies and noticed that many of the hides showed signs of having been caught in traps and snares. With Deafy was Jack Yarzeau who brought in a nine-foot cougar taken in the same area.

Like many other trappers Deafy trapped in many different areas in both the upper and lower McGregor River areas around the stream that still bears his name. Something else that bears mentioning is that he acquired the name Deafy because he was hard of hearing.

During our conversation, Jack Yarzeau had another story about Deafy that emphasizes the importance of these men planning ahead. This event took place when Deafy decided to look over some new area to add to his trapline. "Several warm sunny days had melted the snow. Then a heavy frost came that set up the crust of snow and made it excellent for forest travel. Deafy took this opportunity to explore an area behind a ridge about seven miles from his cabin. He left early in the morning and a couple hours later was looking over this new territory. Some time after noon he came back to the sunny side of the mountain only to find that the crust had melted and would no longer support his weight. Floundering in snow up to his waist, he realized that he had made a terrible mistake by not bringing his snowshoes along. After breaking through the snow crust for a short distance, he realized that he was playing out, so he stopped and built a fire, then decided to camp for the night, and walk out on the frozen crust in the morning." Jack paused for a minute and then went on, "That night a rain storm moved in causing the snow to become even more rotten. Here he was, only a few miles from his cabin, and able to move only a short distance before succumbing to exhaustion.

"He tried in vain to fashion a crude pair of snowshoes, but he had no decent material to work with. With the realization that he did not have warm enough clothing to spend another night in the forests, he decided to try a long shot. He worked his way down into the adjacent creek bottom where he followed the creek. Here he made better progress, but many times he broke through into the icy water and got his legs wet. The water was so unbearably cold that he could only travel a short distance before he was forced to stop and light a fire to warm his feet and legs enough so that they could function. At about eight o'clock that evening he arrived at his cabin so completely exhausted that it took him several days to recover. It had taken him over twelve hours to cover a distance of about two miles."

Jack, like many other trappers and guides of that era, had his run-ins with bears. But the one that stood out in his memory, went like this, "I was walking along the Herrick [Creek] with my dog in late fall when it suddenly took off into the forest at great speed, barking frantically. Normally it would obey me, but for some reason it paid no attention that time. In less than a minute, it came tearing back out of the trees pursued by a grizzly bear with two cubs. Then all hell broke loose. For the next few minutes there was a lot of noise going on."

When it seemed as though Jack was going to leave it at that, I asked, "Did you have to kill her?"

"Yes, there was no way around it." He responded, then added, "Dogs are not always an asset in the woods, you know! Especially if they won't obey."

9

CABIN FEVER

DURING THE BUILDING OF THE GRAND TRUNK PACIFIC railroad and for years after, there were many people living in the forests of British Columbia. There were trappers, prospectors and would-be farmers, as well as loners without identities who minded their own business and hoped others would do the same. We can only wonder how many of them made a careless move or a foolish mistake and paid for it with their lives. Sometimes only a skull or a few bones were found; other times, unidentifiable corpses floated down the rivers.

My father told us about two prospectors who came out to Penny about 1925 after a long stint back in the mountains. They told a story about finding a man's leg bone in a heavy boot on the bank of a creek about 30 miles distant. Word of their discovery reached the authorities and they were ordered to take police back to the scene. A 60-mile hike they had to take for nothing, because nothing else was ever found during their intensive search. This person's fate and identity was forever hidden by the endless forests and mountains, his last rites just the lonely howl of a wolf pack.

While working on a forest fire in 1961, I learned just how easy it was to blend into the wilderness before the modern intensive use of aircraft. I stumbled into the remains of what once was a very well constructed cabin which I guessed must have been built about 1930. When I arrived home, I asked my dad, "Who built that nice cabin by that little lake on the ridge top over there?"

My dad looked at the mountain and then replied, "What cabin? I never knew there was a cabin there!"

Someone had taken a considerable amount of time to construct a fine cabin and clear what appeared to have once been a substantial garden spot only three miles from our home and Dad had been unaware of it. It seems obvious that some of these people went out of their way to avoid others. Some spent so much time in the forests alone that they took leave of their senses and became murderers, suicidals, or people caught just about halfway to nowhere.

A few of these situations are dealt with in the following pages, and they serve to show the daunting tasks the police and game wardens had to face in their endless searches for law-breakers, injured, lost and drowned people. Some stories show the grim reality of days when people were often forced to take the law into their own hands. An example of which follows. It was carried in the *Fort George Herald* dated October 11, 1911:

Man with Gun Goes Hunting Trouble and Finds it

The office of Hamilton and White's livery and dray business on Second Street Monday afternoon looked like a slaughter house, with clotted blood half an inch thick on the floor to the left of the entrance and the front door bespattered with it.

Charlie Hartsell, trapper.

The cause of it all was the silly and unnecessary practice of carrying a gun. It appears that Wm. McEwen, who conducts a second-hand store in the Burns Block on Fourth Street, went into the office, and after seating himself on the couch at the entrance, while Mr. White was occupied at the desk, asked for a rig and stated that he wanted a clean one, with good cushions, rug and a whip, and he would do the driving; but did not state where he wanted to go.

Mr. White informed him that he could have the rig, but it had been a custom to allow no rigs out without a driver.

"Don't you think I can drive," retorted McEwen.

"I do not dispute you," answered White, "but we have found it profitable to allow out no rig without a driver."

This apparently did not suit McEwen, for he is reported to have said, "...that everybody has it in for me in this town."

"I don't think so," returned White. "I gave you oats and hay for your stock in the spring and did not press you for payment. That doesn't look like having it in for you.

The lie was passed, and White, who still was at his desk with his back to McEwen, turned around, and as he did so, noticed McEwen pull out a .32 gun from his inside vest pocket.

Quick as a flash White pinned his wrist and before McEwen could cover White with the weapon, White gave his assailant a staggering blow between the eyes that sent him back to the couch, and in the scramble White took the gun away from McEwen and gave him a trouncing the marks of which he will carry through life.

McEwen has been confined to bed for four days, being unable to appear at court on account of his injuries.

The weapon was given to the constable.

A strange coincidence is that fifteen minutes before the occurrence McEwen was heard to say: "I'll show some of these people," and the butt of the loaded pistol was seen in his inside vest pocket.

McEwen came in over the Blackwater Road early last spring with several wagon loads of furniture and other household articles which he has been gradually disposing of.

The case comes up for trial tonight.

McEwen's penalty was $20 fine and $10 costs.

This next story is one that was whispered about when I was a child. It is from the *Fort George Herald* of May 24, 1913:

Tragedy in the Wilds is Confirmed

Some months ago we published a story which reached us from the construction camps on the upper Fraser, about a gruesome tragedy which centered around two inexperienced Frenchmen who were cut off in the woods, and suffered from the pangs of hunger, until one of them became a maddened fiend and murdered his companion to devour his remains.

The truth of this terrible story is borne out by the arrival in Vancouver of George Horwitz, who visited the scene and verified the facts.

The tragedy was discovered by Mr. P. G. McKenzie, one of a party of surveyors who organized a burial party of six white men and two Indians and who gave Mr. Horwitz photographs of the remains and of the burial party.

Mr. Horwitz was working for a contracting firm at Mile 93 when he first heard vague rumours of the finding of the partly eaten body of a man about 24 miles west of the line near Mile 190. The report was denied by officials, according to the story which Mr. Horwitz tells to a coast contemporary, but when he was leaving the country he encountered Mr. McKenzie and obtained confirmation of the rumours. From Mr. McKenzie and others along the railway route, Mr. Horwitz learned that the two men concerned in the horrifying affair were supposed to have come from Montreal and that somewhere along this grade there is supposed to be a man who knows their identity. According to the information this man was acquainted with one of the two and realized their inability to cope with the adversities of life in the wilderness.

When the men started into the remote region they were without adequate equipment for an ordinary prospecting or hunting trip of short duration, and in spite of warnings given by their acquaintances persisted in the reckless venture of attempting to subsist in the wilds and successfully prosecute a trapping expedition. Trace of the men was lost until the survey party reached the vicinity in which they had erected a crude log cabin as a base for their operations. This cabin was located on a hillside, almost above the timberline and in a region offering but slight opportunities for their chosen pursuit.

When the surveyors reached the cabin they were surprised to note no signs of life and began an investigation. They discovered the frozen and partly dismembered body of one of the trappers half hidden in the snow. The body was frightfully mutilated and there was a deep gash in the back of the head. On the door of the cabin was scrawled in French the almost illegible inscription, "Starved for nine days. Went crazy." No supplies of any kind were visible. The men had been without a stove, but in the center of the hut were the remains of a campfire. Nearby was a rusty frying pan in which the men were startled to find the remains of human ribs.

The surveyors obtained boards from their camp and buried the remains in a rough box which they constructed, marking the spot with a cross.

Search failed to disclose any trace of the man who killed his companion, and the surveyors believe he wandered half-mad through the timber until he perished from exposure.

THE FOLLOWING STORY DEMONSTRATES THE NATURE OF some of the men that walked this area in past generations. This took place in Johnson's Hotel with its famous 70 foot-long bar, located in South Fort George. It was taken from the *Fort George Herald* of May 31, 1913:

A man named Kilpatrick, a giant in stature and strength, precipitated a small riot in the Northern hotel last Thursday night by refusing to leave the bar room when ordered to by the house policeman, Charlie Wylie. Wylie, who is also a big man, closed with the scow-man and a battle of giants opened fast and furious. Kilpatrick was thrown out about the time the police appeared on the scene. He resisted arrest and a free-for-all fight started. Chief Daunt and his men had great difficulty in preventing a serious riot among the foreigners who closed in on them, and they were forced to draw their guns, but handled the difficult situation with credit. Kilpatrick was taken to the lockup. He was fined fifty dollars or three months in jail, on a charge of creating a disturbance.

This Charlie Wylie was truly a unique individual. In assisting a peace officer in an attempted arrest, a crazed gambler shot him through a hotel door. Mortally wounded, Charlie broke down the door and shot the man dead before succumbing to his own wounds. Many people simply were not cut out for living in the wilderness. For some, a solitary stay in the wilds was a one-way ticket to disaster, as evidenced in the following article from *The Citizen* of September 9, 1921:

Lives a Hermit's Life in Northern Wilds

Travellers recently returned from McLeod Lake bring word that George Haas, a former resident of this city, is living the life of a hermit in a tumbledown shack about twelve miles from McLeod. He is said to be partly demented and has various hallucinations, one of which is a long-distance telephone whereby he is able to call up Vancouver, Edmonton and various other district points at will. A cluster of empty cans hung in the shack produces the Jangle, and he is then in direct communication with outside points.

Haas is a German and a former Prussian guardsman. He left the city for the wilds shortly after war broke out, fearing internment. Travellers say his clothes are filthy and in tatters and he subsists entirely upon what small animals and fish he is able to capture.

And again in the Prince George newspaper *The Leader* of June 2, 1922:

Another Wild Man Reported Hereabouts
Type of Primitive Man, Said to Resemble a Bear Flees at Sight of Fellow Man

The following story, bearing a Prince George date line, has been going the rounds of the western press recently. It shows the awful effects of homebrew on the mind of some rural residents. Here is the story of the local 'wild man':

How near does a human being resemble a bear, or how near does a bear resemble a human being? Is a busy question just at present in the Prince George district of British Columbia, owing to rumours of a 'wild man' running at large in the Chief Lake district. His description given by those who have seen him is such that he is easily mistaken for a bear at first sight. He narrowly escapes the attention of the rifle of every homesteader, especially during this time when the she bear and her cubs are out, hungry and desperate, in search of food.

This 'wild man' has been seen in different localities lately. Those who got close enough to see it was a human and not a marauding animal, describe him as a type of the primitive cave man or tree-top dweller; huge in stature, his few rags streaming, and he flees as a deer when seen.

He is evidently a white man, according to them. This part of BC has had its 'wild men' running at large, more or less, ever since the advent of the Grand Trunk Pacific, supposed to have been working on railway construction, afterwards squatting on the wild lands abounding in this district, until they in turn become 'wild' themselves, according to the remoteness from supplies or from other human companionship.

～≫

ANOTHER PERFECT EXAMPLE OF SOMEONE SPENDING TOO much time alone and not being able to handle it, was taken from *The Citizen* of Sept. 11, 1941:

When a grey-bearded, tattered, ancient trapper in a patched brown and yellow mackinaw shirt arrived in Sinclair Mills Monday, nobody realized a great reformer had hit town. Shortly afterwards, however, equipped with a messianic mania and a large and impressive knife, he started in to reform the town in earnest.

At 5 p.m., Sgt. George Clark received a call here from Sinclair Mills that the old chap, who hailed from Hansard, was conducting a one man reign of terror. However, by the time Sgt. Clark and Const. W. Smith arrived there after a fast auto and speeder trip, the maniac had been overpowered and disarmed and was strapped to a stretcher. He was brought to Prince George by train, committed, and taken to Essondale by plane Tuesday, Const. Thomas taking him down.

Among the people that the wilderness beat down are the great number that simply went missing, and the total is nothing short of staggering — trappers and prospectors especially. The number of so-called suicides among trappers was very high, although many of the so-called suicides were suspect because furs had gone missing.

Just a small example of what the police faced is indicated in the following headlines taken from *The Citizen* over a short period of time in the '30s:

Fight For Cabin Ends in Murder and in Suicide

Provincial Game Warden Shot Near Lillooet

Francis Gott Shot in Both Legs

**Prospector Henry Derby Killed When
Snow Laden Tent Collapses**

Hixon Miner Frozen to Death Near His Cabin

**Constable Boys Travels 600 Miles
to Investigate Trapper Suicide**

Veteran Trapper Jack Weisner Froze Feet

Body of Prospector Robert Booth Found on Trail

Trapper Shot by Hidden Foe

Prospectors Fight Duel on Northern Trail

Trapper Charlie Spencer Dies in Lonely Cabin

Suicide Follows Confession of Double Murder

These headlines suffice to show that the police certainly had their hands full.

10

ADVENTURERS

$\mathcal{S}$OON AFTER THE STEAMER *ENTERPRISE* CLIMBED THE FRASER through Fort George, in the 1880s to be exact, there was another adventurous soul that followed. This man was Twelve-foot Davis, and he left a legacy that is an outstanding example of the courage and tenacity some of these pioneers possessed. His story was carried in the *Fort George Herald* on Jan. 21, 1911:

A Born Transportation Man

Years ago there lived and worked on the Fraser River between Quesnel and Giscome Portage a born transportation man. This man was Twelve-Foot Davis. He derived this name in the Williams' Creek [Barkerville Gold rush] diggings through having discovered and staked a 12-foot fraction that ran $1000 to the foot. Today, amongst us at Fort George, may be noticed an old bent Indian, whiskered and decent looking and who by every moral right should be chief of his tribe, and would be, did he long for earthly honors. This was Twelve-Foot Davis' right hand man whom he trusted for years to steer his boats in perilous places. He is probably a man who knows more about steering with a sweep or paddle than any living man on the mighty Peace and Fraser Rivers and their tributaries. An old Hudson's Bay Co. *engagé* and trapper from time immemorial, with the honor of that honorable company deep in his soul, he is regarded by men of the North who know him as a great man and the greatest judge of swift water imaginable.

During the unrest in the Northwest and Manitoba during the Riel Rebellion the Hudson's Bay Co. shipped flour to Fort Vermilion and other lower Peace River posts from Victoria, thence up the Fraser River to Quesnel, by steamer, pack horse and freight team. From Quesnel, Twelve-Foot Davis took the contract to land the freight at the lower Peace River posts. To this end three boats were constructed with a capacity of 15,000 pounds each, towed and manned by both Lillooet Indians and those of the upper Fraser and Nechako. Three trips a season were made for three years to Giscome Portage.

During the autumn of each year 45,000 pounds were portaged on Indian backs and horses across to Summit Lake from the landing of Giscome annually. Three scows were constructed at the lake, carrying 15,000 pounds each and carrying five horses distributed on them for use at Rocky Mountain Canyon, Peace River, which is impassable. Here the scows were abandoned, and the cargo packed around the canyon, a distance of 15 miles to rafts below, on which the rest of the long journey was completed.

On Davis' last season on this contract he built the largest boats ever hauled by men on the river, carrying 36,000 pounds each. Davis started from Quesnel with a cargo of flour in the spring. At Fort George he picked up 15 canoes for lightening purposes. On arrival at Giscome Portage he hauled these large boats as well as the cargoes across the portage with the aid of four horses and the Indians. Only a fortnight was taken to accomplish this. An Indian's load of flour was 150 pounds, and he went half the distance (four miles) across the portage without a rest. However, it was difficult to keep the boys from carrying more, as they wished to outdo one another. Reloading and after crossing Summit Lake they discovered that there was not sufficient water to carry the large boat. Davis, never at a loss, lightened her up with his 15 canoes and built an immense dam, letting the water back up overnight. In the morning the dam was quickly broken and the flood carried Davis and his fleet into deep water again and so on down the Crooked River into McLeod Lake; thence into the Pack River, where two more scows were constructed and the canoes abandoned.

From the Pack the scows were taken into the Parsnip, thence into the Peace, through the dangerous Finlay and Pack Pass Rapids and on to Rocky Mountain Canyon — through which no boat can pass — and then lined through and over the portage road to rafts below.

The three smaller boats were brought back onto the Fraser River, but the largest one with a sack of flour in its stern, was sent intentionally to destruction through the canyon.

WHY THEY SENT THE BOAT THROUGH THE CANYON IS
unknown, perhaps just to see what would happen, to show why the
canyon was impassable.

From the earliest years, there has been a number of extraordinary
people who have walked this land; people who stand out from the
crowd, so to speak. One such person in my estimation, was a trapper named Jack Evans. A kindly man, I remember the many times he
brought chocolate bars to us when we were children, and the countless stories he told us about his experiences in the forests he knew and
loved so dearly.

Born in England in 1867 he settled in Ontario for a time, then
moved with his father to Manitoba before heading west to BC. In
1895 he arrived in the Fort George area, then moved to Barkerville
for a while before returning to Fort George where he spent the next
several years trapping the area north toward Salmon River.

In 1908 he went up the Fraser River to Dewey where he took
over a trapline that had been abandoned by Karl Moxley, who had
made his fortune in the timber staking days of 1905 and had given
up chasing fur for the easier life of a timber baron.

This was a trapline over 100 miles long, a portion of which
stretched up the Big Salmon River, and people were greatly impressed
with it. Quesnel's *Cariboo Observer* in its May 22, 1909 edition called
it "the longest and best equipped trapline in British Columbia."

It was along this line that Jack came upon two young men in dire
need of assistance. Of American origin, they had left Vancouver that
summer intent on spending a year of adventure in the wilderness.
Their inexperience was obvious, for the roof of their shelter leaked
profusely with the result that all their supplies, including the flour, had
spoiled. Their clothes and bedding were damp, and the smell of
mildew permeated the place. Jack made them a meal, then snowshoed back to the mouth of the river where he kept one of several
food caches. After bringing back enough supplies to nurse the two
men back to health, he then helped them out to South Fort George
where they eventually made their way home.

Jack was a quiet sincere gentleman who, even at the age of 80, stood straight as a soldier and was respected by all who knew him. He was, according to my mother, my namesake and I have always considered it an honour to have been named after him.

Whenever he felt lonely he would come to our home for a visit, and I can still remember listening to his stories of adventure in the forests he loved so dearly. After a few hours of being around all us children, he would beat a hasty retreat back across the river to his cabin, no doubt giving praise to the almighty that he was a bachelor. Some of the stories he told us are held in our memories and I hope that time has not distorted them too much.

Of all the predicaments he got into in the forests, the worst occurred one November day when he carried a heavy load of supplies into an area where he was going to lay out a new piece of

One of the early Fort George trappers, Jack Evans. c. 1940.

trapline. Just a little while before dark, he stopped at the top of a steep draw where he decided to spend the night. A stream could be heard down in the bottom of the draw, so he leaned his pack against a tree, took his billy can, and started down to get some water with which to make tea. As he made his way down the steep slope, the going got tough and the stream was much farther down then he had anticipated. By the time he found the stream and got the pail of water, a rainstorm hit that quickly turned to snow. With the snow came darkness so that by the time he reached the top of the draw, he had no idea where his pack was. Now he was in one hell of a fix: wet from sweating while carrying a heavy pack all day, he was in dire need of dry clothes, food and most of all, a fire. His matches were all in waterproof containers in his pack, along with his axe and bug. For about an hour, he wandered around the top of the draw in a raging blizzard, feeling around the bottom of trees for his pack before he luckily put his hand right on it. A few minutes later he had a roaring fire going and the world seemed a much brighter place.

Jack had another scare one December day when he fell through river ice up to his waist. He quickly got back into the forest and built a good hot fire to dry himself out. Being a woods-wise man, he always kept a good supply of fire starter in his pack, be it kindling, birch bark, lichen or whatever else was available where he travelled. Candles were always carried for his bugs, were also excellent fire starters.

A story I used to ask him to tell over and over was about a fight between a moose and a wolf pack. This occurred while he was following his trapline one winter day and came upon a place where a wolf pack had surrounded a moose. What made this encounter different was that this moose didn't run. Instead it kept its hind end between two big cedar trees that grew close together. At some point one of the wolves had grown impatient and had attacked from the front. Its flattened-out carcass was lying in the snow and the obviously defeated pack had moved on. The moose was seen feeding a short distance away, seemingly unconcerned.

On one visit to our house he told us a story about how he had got in a fight with a skunk that he found hanging around his cabin. During the altercation the skunk sprayed and Jack said it almost got him. That wasn't the whole truth, though, for a person only had to get within 10 feet of him to know that the skunk had scored a near direct hit.

Jack was a very honest person who kept his word and expected others to do the same. I'm thinking about a time when he loaned a pitchfork to a neighbour who promised to return it in a few days. The pitchfork was never returned and Jack summed it all up by saying, "If a man's word is no good, then he's no good either."

Jack also used to recall the time from his Barkerville days where he saw a game of Russian roulette played, and he had another story about walking through the mountains from Penny to Barkerville, a distance of almost 60 miles, to attend a wake where he saw booze being poured into a corpse.

He also told us that he used to smoke meat by hanging large chunks in his chimney where it would form a hard crust several inches thick. Inside, the meat was cured and excellent.

In 1912 Jack took out a pre-emption in the Tonequah Creek area where he became a rancher for a time. And then in 1926 he applied for a crown grant on the property across the Fraser River from Penny where he trapped for several years and eventually retired.

Perhaps my fondest memories of him are the times he brought buckets full of strawberries to our sports days. This was just one of many kindnesses he showed, for it was well known that he gave money to people in need.

I also recall the time I walked down to the river with him and watched as he loaded his groceries into the cedarstrip canoe he had built himself. He pushed off and paddled up river, a man in his seventies who easily overpowered the strong river current.

One day in late autumn when he was visiting us, he made a strange statement: "I guess they'll be putting me in a box pretty soon now." These were very prophetic words, as we were about to find out that winter. For he didn't think he was going to die — he *knew* he was going to die.

During a cold snap in January 1948, Joe Pastor, who lived across the Fraser River from Jack, noticed there was no smoke coming from his chimney. He crossed the river ice to his cabin and found him dead. He had frozen to death, and there was not a stick of firewood anywhere on the place. For some reason he had not put up his winter's supply of firewood and not wanting to be a burden to anyone, had not mentioned it; for if he had, an abundant supply of firewood would have appeared on his doorstep in very short order.

I was 14 years old when he passed away, and I felt a deep sense of loss. Like other guides and trappers, he was one of my heroes when I was a young lad, one of those strange men who disappeared into the forests to become one with nature. I felt that something mysterious and precious was gone from the south side of the river, much more than just "Jack Evans — trapper — dead at the age of 81."

The following summer several of us crossed the Fraser River to his cabin where we were in for a pleasant surprise: upstairs in his cabin we found many letters on the floor. Since we were unaware that he

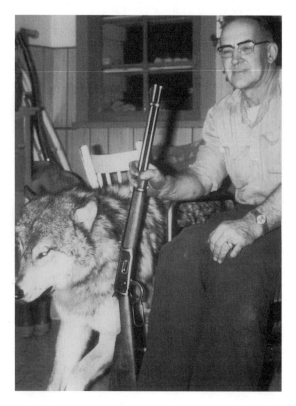

John Perry with the leader of the wolf pack, 1955.

had been corresponding with anyone, curiosity made us open them. The letters were all the same: "We thank you again for your donation to the Red Cross." "We thank you once again for your donation to the Red Cross." The floor was covered with them.

It seemed so strange to me that the man who gave so much to others could not bring himself to ask one favor in return.

These next stories were told to me by John Perry and his brother Miles who still reside at their ranch on the Willow River 20 miles east of Prince George where this story unfolded. Now in their twilight years, these two men have many memories that they have been willing to share. To the unbelieving, I would just say that the grit inherent in this family becomes readily apparent when one watches John, in his wheelchair, cutting firewood with a chainsaw or splitting firewood with an axe.

As good a place as any to start is in 1914, when their father Edwin Perry arrived in Prince George with the Grand Trunk Pacific Railroad, employed as a cement engineer. Upon completion of his work, he was offered a similar job in China, which he refused. With his wife he moved into a small house in Prince George and bought a quarter section of land on the Willow River where the family still resides.

In May 1916 Edwin purchased a team of horses, moved into a tent on the homestead, and began clearing land. One morning he went to harness the horses, but they wouldn't cooperate. Instead they bolted and ran away into the forest with Edwin in hot pursuit. This was a financial loss that Edwin could not bear so he had only one option; he had to catch the horses. He returned home where he gathered up a small packsack with a bit of food and a .22 calibre rifle, then headed back into the forest. This was the 14th of May.

All along the Willow watershed Edwin followed the horses, along George Creek, Narrow Lake, Stony Lake and up toward Bowron Lakes. Often close, he was never able to get a rope on them. All through the summer months he trailed them, living on grouse, rabbits, fish, berries and whatever else nature provided. At last the snow forced him out of the mountains and he reached civilization by coming out at Barkerville. Here he contacted the police and was told that a stranger with horses had managed to capture two other horses just a few days earlier. The description of the horses matched perfectly, so the search was aborted.

From Barkerville Edwin walked out to Quesnel where he caught a steamer back to Prince George. Having given him up for dead, his wife was shocked to see a heavily bearded man whom she mistook for a beggar suddenly turn into her husband. The date was November 27th, he had been gone six and a half months.

The Perry brothers also tell the story of a trail that used to cross their property. When they were children, their father used to tell them it was called the Dolimar Trail. It was cut down into the ground at least six inches from where the many travellers and their animals had walked. Fitting in with this story, was another told to them by pioneer Albert Hubbard of Giscome, who told them that he had hauled a large roll of cable up the Willow River with dog teams many years earlier. The cable was obviously used to construct a bridge across the Willow River that stayed there for many years, which Miles, the senior Perry had seen in his youth. This bridge was about five miles downstream from the Highway 16 bridge. It was built from the three-quarter inch cable and had six-inch poles tied side by side all the way across. This river crossing was a must for the trail which went east and branched; one trail led to Hansard, and a branch of it went on to Bear River as shown on the river mileages [See appendices]. The other branch turned southeast and went along between the Willow River and the Bowron River to Barkerville.

An Indian used to work for the Perrys when Miles and John were young men. He told them that when he was a lad of 14 years, a man called Cataline hired him in Fort George to help him take a pack train along this trail to Barkerville, which he did. He also said that this Cataline had about 20 mules and mostly black men for trail hands.

For those who don't know who Cataline was, I think it's safe to say that he was the most famous packer in the history of the province. He packed to Hazelton, the Omineca, Cassiar, and Barkerville, among other places. Born Jean Caux, he earned the nickname Cataline and it stuck with him. Another thing that this Indian told the Perrys was that Cataline used to buy a bottle of booze and pour it over his head, something that has been established by other sources. I find it most interesting to think that this famous packer at one time used to frequent our area of the province, too.

As for the cable bridge across the Willow River, Miles says that settlers tore it out in the '30s and used the cable for a bucket style crossing over the river at a different spot. The Perrys add another footnote to this story by saying that when they were hired to haul supplies with horses along the Willow River in the '30s, they found portions of this trail and could still see where three-foot fir down trees had been chopped out with axes, many years earlier.

The Perrys have another story that I feel deserves telling. They received an unexpected visitor one winter day during the Great Depression. This man had shinnied across the Willow River on a down tree and trudged several miles through the snow in a desperate effort to save his wife and unborn child. On an isolated homestead, living on little more than turnips, they were in desperate need of medical attention because his wife was unable to deliver.

Frank Cooke, Sr., guide and outfitter. c. 1930.

John saddled a horse and rode into Prince George, a distance of about 20 miles, only to find the doctor unwilling to leave because of his duty to other patients. John rode his horse to the police station and informed the attending officer of the medical emergency. Bidding John to follow, the policeman led the way back to the doctor and told him, "Get your bag; you're going with this man!" A taxi took the doctor out as far as the Giscome turnoff where it got stuck. The doctor then climbed on the horse behind John and doubled the rest of the way back to the Perry Ranch.

With bag in hand, the good doctor followed him through the forest, across the down tree over the open Willow River to the homestead where the delivery was a complete success.

One of the most indomitable spirits to ever grace this area, was described in the May 8, 1910 edition of the *Cariboo Observer:*

> "One of the most remarkable trips made throughout the Northern Interior of British Columbia this year was that taken by M. M. Bowman. He is a chemist at the Dupont Powder Works of Pinole, Cal., and is on a pleasure jaunt and making a study with pictures of wild animal life. Mr. Bowman left Kamloops in April and packed along his camera and provisions up through the North Thompson country to Tête Jaune Cache. Here he constructed a canoe for himself and floated down the Fraser River to Fort George, where he again took the trail last week for the Fraser Lake District. He will then go overland back to Vancouver via the Bella Coola Valley. The remarkable part of the trip is that Mr. Bowman has but one arm and is travelling without companionship. En route he received the good wishes and bon voyage of all whom he met, and all friends wish him a successful completion of his trip."

11

THE JENSENS

IN 1911 ERNEST JENSEN LEFT HIS NATIVE NORWAY AND CAME to Canada. A few months later, he moved to the Dome Creek area where he eventually took out a pre-emption right along the Fraser River. In 1912 and 1913, he was hired on as a hunter for the Grand Trunk Pacific Railway. He was one of several hunters who were hired to help supply food for the many employees on the bridge and grade construction. His brother Einar arrived in 1914 and Arna or Arne, the youngest brother, arrived in 1921. All three men became trappers and guides and were generally accepted as being among the best in the business.

Although moose were present in the area since about 1900, Ernest spent a whole year in the forests before he seeing one. The moose were working their way south at about eight to ten miles per year. It wasn't long before they were in great abundance, and as some put

Dome Creek Grand Trunk Pacific hunters. Ernest Jensen is third from left. c. 1913.

it, "This wasn't moose overflow; this was a real migration." Caribou were in abundance and it was common to see small herds in every mountain valley.

These men were lucky enough to get into the guiding business when, as Arne put it, "quality was placed far above quantity." It seems difficult to believe that even back in the '20s, they charged up to $2000 per man for a three-week hunt. Included among Arne's many satisfied hunters was the son of Alexander Graham Bell, who left with a fine caribou trophy.

Although I knew the Jensens for many years, it was not until the 1960s and 1970s that I wrote down their many forest adventures that spanned a period of 50 years. Arne ran a string of 20 horses which he used to pack men and supplies far into the headwaters of the McGregor River and into the Alberta Boundary area. Among the animals that he supplied to his hunters were mountain sheep, mountain goat, caribou, grizzlies, black bears, and moose. "Are you aware of the experiments being made in Yellowstone Park where they have found that all the grizzlies go to their dens on the same day?" I questioned.

"All the sows and all the black bears seemed to disappear on the same day, the day that the first heavy snows covered the valley bottoms. Snow that just covered the mountains would not make them den. You must understand that this did not apply to boar grizzlies, as it was common to see them or their tracks in December and again in February. In one winter I found five moose that were definitely killed by grizzlies. All were bulls, in fact, all the grizzly-killed moose that I ever found were bulls. This leaves me to wonder if it was just coincidence or if the bears could possibly be selective," he replied.

"Ole Hansen, who guided 50 miles downriver from you, told me that the majority of bear-killed moose he found were cows." I mentioned.

"Well, maybe the answer to that is quite simple: maybe there were more cow moose where he was and more bulls where I was, because I was trapping at a much higher elevation."

"Did the grizzlies like to make their kills out on the river, the way wolves do?" I asked.

"No! That's a strange thing. The moose seemed to escape by running out on the river ice, as the bears would not follow. They just seemed to admit defeat. Yet the wolves seemed to prefer to make their kills on the ice. I don't know, I never could make any sense out of that."

"In all the years you spent in the woods, Arne, how many grizzlies did you shoot?" I questioned.

"Only one that I can remember. I was following my trapline trail — it was in October — when I noticed something moving on the trail a short distance ahead. I stopped to look for a moment and realized it was a two or three-year-old grizzly. It was crouched down low like a cat, sneaking toward me. I slipped the rifle off my back and shot it in the forehead at about 20 feet. It dropped dead, lucky for me, because I was only carrying a .22."

"Did you ever have any problem with bears around your cabins or tents?" I asked.

"Many times. I remember a time in late fall when I visited a line cabin that I hadn't been at for some time. When I got close, I noticed a window had been broken. I snuck up and looked in the window and saw a black bear on my bunk. He had packed a whole bunch of willows and boughs in there and made a den right on my bunk. It's a good thing that I noticed the broken window or else I would have walked right into it when I opened the door. You see, the door had swung shut again. Well, he wasn't paying any rent and he wasn't helping with the chores; so he left, dragged out on the end of a rope."

"I remember the pictures you had of a grizzly bear eating beaver carcasses right beside your cabin.

"Do you still have them, Arne?"

"I sure do. That grizzly used to stay about 80 to 100 feet from the cabin. It wouldn't come any closer. But if I started walking toward it, it would chase me right back into the cabin. That could have been the same bear that came back a couple years later and took a slab of bacon out of the meat house. It came back another three times before it quit."

"What is your opinion of the wolf poisoning program?" I asked.

"I have to tell you that I was very critical of it. I think it killed far more than just wolves. Before the poisoning took place it was common for me to see 40 to 50 eagles feeding on drowned moose in one trip along my line in spring. Later, I travelled my entire line and only noticed one. I also think that there was little if any change in the moose and deer populations after the wolves were gone."

"These eagles you mentioned. Were they golden or bald eagles?" I asked.

"Both. And you know they sure added a touch of comedy to trapline life in late spring when they used to feed on beaver carcasses until they were so full that they could not fly. Many times I watched them attempt to take flight and have to give up. A couple times, I saw them land with a splash in the river and have to swim for it. This swimming, of course was accomplished by using their wings as oars."

Remembering a story I had heard about an accident that had happened to him, I asked: "Did you ever get into any dangerous binds out there, Arne?"

"Well, I always tried to put safety first, but some things are beyond our control. For example, I remember the time I was out in the woods shooting squirrels with my .22 when I got a blow-back that gave me real bad powder burns in my eye. I was in a great deal of difficulty and in extreme pain but I managed to make it to one of my line cabins. When I got there I fashioned a poultice out of tea leaves and applied it to my eye. This seemed to help some, but the pain was almost unbearable."

Arne shook his head to make the point, then continued, "For several days I laid in the cabin before I finally decided to try to make it to the main cabin. It was snowing lightly as I made my way along the trail until I got about half-way, then the sun came out unbearably bright on the fresh snow. Even though I had made a mask of sorts for shade, my sore and watery left eye could not stand the strain and suddenly everything went dark."

Again he paused, showing considerable emotion. "Never have I known such a feeling of helplessness. I was miles from my nearest cabin without a trace of vision. My brothers were not expecting me out for another month, so help was out of the question. As I sat there in the snow, I realized that there was only one option, and that was to use the gun on myself. Just as the darkest thoughts crossed my mind, I caught a glimpse of light and this gave me enough hope to hang on. After a couple hours the vision in my left eye cleared enough for me to make my way to the main cabin where I had an abundance of food and firewood. I went to get medical attention and it was months before that eye settled down. Now the last few years it has started to bother me again."

Arne's first problem had been the result of an accident; the second one was caused by a quirk of nature. "I was trapping up near Jarvis Creek one winter when the weather went from being warm to 30 degrees below zero. It didn't take very long until there was an ice jam at the canyon [Eight-Mile Canyon]. The water backed up slowly and covered the surrounding lowlands and I was chased for over a mile before I found a spot that was high enough above the rising water for me to spend the night. The next day I carried on

Arne Jensen in Danish Navy. c. 1920.

to one of my line cabins where I found the water at window level and all the firewood afloat. I knew that I had to keep moving, so I was forced to continue on downriver toward the next cabin. In one spot I was forced to walk through a layer of water that was up above my knees, and I wasn't sure that the ice was strong enough to support my weight without snowshoes so I was forced to wear them. By the time I reached the other bank of the river, my snowshoes weighed about 50 pounds each. To make matters even worse, a strong wind was blowing that froze both of my legs before I reached the cabin. After the ice jam broke free I went to Prince George and received medical attention, and it was a full year before my legs healed completely."

"You must have had some scares from animals in all those years, didn't you?" I asked.

"I can tell you about one that sure got my heart beating faster." Arne told me. "I was trapping beaver far up the McGregor in May when it happened. I was following the riverbank heading for a line cabin when I came upon fresh grizzly tracks going in the same direction as me. I was a little excited at the size of the tracks, so I put a

Falls and log-jam at Eight-mile Canyon on the McGregor River. A long-time navigational hazard, the log-jam finally cleared itself out naturally during spring high waters.

shell in the barrel, just to be safe. Well, I walked for about half a mile and then came around a bend in the river and there was the bear. It was crouched down in some alders right beside the trail, waiting for me. I felt shivers running up and down my spine, but I took aim and fired, and then I was surprised to find that the bear didn't move. I finally worked up enough nerve to move ahead slowly, with my gun at the ready, and found that the grizzly was in fact a moose hide that the wolves had dragged into the alders. It fooled me completely in the fading light."

"Any stories about watching wildlife?" I questioned.

"I recall sitting on a mountain one day watching a grizzly bathing in a small lake a short distance below me. For over an hour it alternately bathed and soaked itself and this was done by the bear standing on its hind legs and dipping itself up and down, just like a person does when trying to adjust to cold water.

"On another trip, Ernest and I sat on a mountain peak watching a big grizzly eating on a moose it had killed down by a little stream. After eating, it stretched out right on top of the remains of the moose and just laid there, taking life easy. I guess we watched for about an hour before the wind shifted and took our scent to the bear. All at once it exploded up off the carcass like it had been stabbed in the belly. Then, with a few good leaps, it disappeared into a thicket. It came back later to finish eating the carcass.

"Grizzlies always cleaned up every last bit of a carcass unless they were bothered by man." Arne went on. "They should not be compared to wolves that often waste a lot of meat. On the other hand, a lot of meat was wasted by the smaller packs in real cold weather because they just couldn't chew it. You know, in 30 below weather you can hardly chop it with an axe."

"Do you believe that wolves only take the sick and the weak?" I asked.

"That just isn't true, but for those who insist on believing it, let's remember that delivering cows and newborn calves are definitely among the weak. When the snow is real deep a light crust will fully support the wolves while their prey flounders neck deep. In those conditions there is no escape."

"What's the largest number of wolves you've ever seen in a pack?"

"Well, Ernest watched two large packs as they met in a big meadow in February. They spent about an hour sizing each other up before going their separate ways. He tried his best to count them and figured there was a total of about 80. A few days later, I saw one of these packs on a big meadow and counted 42, the largest pack we had ever seen or heard of."

"I wonder why there is such a difference in pack size." I mused.

"In the deep snow conditions of the upper river, it seemed that the ideal pack size was between 20 and 30 animals." Arne went on, "This allowed the pack to be able to travel long distances when necessary, even through deep snow conditions by constant rotation of lead trail-breakers. This also gave them the ability to eat a whole moose at one feeding, for when the meat would freeze rock-hard in sub-zero temperatures, it would dry out and not be fit to eat after a while. Then it would surely be wasted."

"Ever have wolves follow you?" I asked.

"Several times we had packs follow us, howling continually, and we thought this was a form of entertainment for them because they never tried to harm us. And this only happened in winter. In fact, I never heard of it happening to anyone except in winter."

"Any other thoughts about wolves?" I asked.

"All through the years we found where a lone wolf would follow a few days behind the packs picking up scraps left from their kills. We thought that they might be deposed leaders sent into exile by a new leader, and nature's way of introducing new blood into the packs. Another thing I would like to mention: it was interesting to walk over to where a large pack of wolves had just passed. If the snow was real deep, the wolves would walk in single file in the same trail and it would appear that only a few wolves had gone by. If a person didn't know, they would never guess that 30 wolves had walked there."

Arne beamed as he recalled a special memory. "One winter evening I was busy skinning out some fur and a wolf howled so close to the cabin that I actually jumped. I went outside to investigate and there on a bar by the river sat this wolf, bathed in moonlight, howling at the strange light in its domain. Though it was only 50 yards away it seemed to sense that it was not in danger. For several minutes it sat there and I couldn't help but feel that it was singing just for me. Next morning I went for a look and found that a large pack had waited a little further up the river while this one wolf had come down to sing me a song. You know, of all my memories of the woods, I think that one is the most special."

After Arne moved into Dome Creek, I used to visit him occasionally and I always enjoyed his frank observations of nature. On one visit I asked him what he thought the reason was for the decline of the caribou populations. For several minutes he sat in silence and then said, "I don't know."

"Do you think that the moose had any bearing on it?" I asked.

"I can't see how. They don't even eat the same kind of food, and yet the caribou did start going down hill shortly after the moose arrived. Probably the wolves were more responsible than anything else, I mean they sure killed a lot of them."

"Did you ever have any problem with wolves bothering your horses back there in the mountains." I wondered.

"Not once, in all the years we were back there. Ernest raised several colts back there and on occasion we would see where wolves had walked by only a short distance from them, but they never bothered them. It was sure something to see how they would get the moose, though, they took a lot of them on the ice in winter. Wolverines, too, would sometimes drive deer out on the river ice and kill them."

"Did you manage to catch many wolves when you were trapping?" I queried.

"Well, I remember one interesting day. In some spots along my line I used to set two traps just far enough apart so that a small animal could not reach them both, yet a larger animal like a coyote or wolverine, could. Once they were caught in two traps, their chances of escape were greatly reduced. As I walked along the line to check one of these double sets, I saw that a pack of wolves had walked ahead of me straight toward it. When I got to the set I found a wolf in each trap. After skinning them out, I set the traps again, hoping to catch something else on their carcasses. On the next trip around the line I found that a wolverine had avoided both traps and had taken both carcasses up a very steep cut bank, back into the forest. I followed it for over a mile before I gave up, 'cause I felt that any animal that was willing to work that hard for its meal should be left to eat in peace.

"Another thing," Arne went on. "These wolverine have to be the most tenacious animal in the woods. At least half of the wolverines we caught through the years had porcupine quills in them somewhere or other, and about 20 per cent of them were blind in one eye. Some had a face full of quills, yet it seemed to be business as usual."

"All those quills in their bodies sure must have made them miserable." I suggested.

"I don't think it makes any difference." Arne said jokingly. "They're miserable anyway."

Ernest was a witness to a knock-em-down fight between two boar grizzlies. It happened in his later years when he was employed as a lookout observer for the BC Forest Service on Dome Mountain. In vivid detail he described the fight to listening rangers and their families who sat riveted to their radios like spectators at a boxing match.

Einar and Ernest Jensen above timberline. c. 1930.

Much like a boxing match, the two bears would stop for a rest and then go at it again while the sow stood off to the side waiting the outcome of what for her was a no-lose situation. Finally the bears were lost to view, and the winner — which there surely must have been — was unknown.

The late Bill Haws, who worked for CN Railways until his retirement in 1968, told me about a guiding trip he went on with Einar Jensen up the Ptarmigan Creek in 1926: "When we reached the far end of Einar's line, we came to a mountain that he claimed always produced a grizzly. As soon as we arrived, Einar made a very small fire, then put a full pan of bacon on to fry. We all moved off to one side, while the updrafts took the smell up the mountainside. Within an hour, out came a bear with his nose in gear and the hunter had his grizzly. When I asked Einar how he came to find out about this trick, he said. 'By almost getting my back scratched one morning when I was preparing breakfast'."

"You did a lot of guiding, Arne, what are some of your memories of that?"

"Well, I sure remember one hunter that caused me an unbelievable amount of trouble. This man had a habit of leaving camp and not telling anyone. Several times I warned him of the danger of getting lost or injured but it didn't help. Anyway, I was making breakfast one morning when I heard several shots in the distance. I looked in this fellow's tent and he was not there, so I took off on the run in the direction the shots came from. A little while later I heard a couple more shots echo through the ridges and then I caught up with the hunter who was more than just a little shook up. He had walked a ways from camp and met a grizzly, and then fired several shots and knocked the bear down. He right away went and began skinning the bear and after he had removed the hide from part of the hind quarters, the bear regained consciousness, got up and started walking away through the trees. That hunter said it was the strangest sight imaginable, the back end of the bear showing white while the skinned out portion of the hide dragged alongside. The only good thing I can say about that hunter is that after getting over his initial shock, he had the courage to go after the bear and finish it off." Arne then grinned and added, "The back end of that bear hide looked more like a pair of pants than a bear hide. He sure made a mess of it."

"Did you ever have trouble with bears bothering your campsites, Arne?"

"Yes. If you camp out a lot, you're bound to. Ernest and I spent part of one summer cutting fire access trails for the BC Forest Service up Ptarmigan Creek. Now and then we would take a few days off and go home for a rest. Well, it was after our days off that we returned to camp to find that bears had played havoc with our tent. It was totally wrecked from where the bears had walked in and out at random. The water bucket and stove pipe were flattened out, both sleeping bags were gone, and a trail of sugar and flour could be seen leading off into the forest. After following the trail for a while, we found one sleeping bag stretched out over some bushes like it had been placed out to dry. Then we came upon the flour bag with a little flour left in the bottom. Back near the remains of the tent, we found the other sleeping bag all rolled up inside an air mattress with neither one damaged. Well, we were a long way from civilization and did not want to walk out again, so we used the remaining flour and caught enough fish to survive until the job was done. And yes, there was fantastic fishing above the falls on Ptarmigan Creek in the '30s.

"I should also mention that every time we had our camps bothered by bears, it was always mothers and cubs."

"I meant to ask you before, what was the largest number of caribou you ever ran into in one herd?"

"Probably about 50, but it's hard to tell if you meet them in the timber. I mean there could be way more than you see. But Einar ran into a real big herd back in the '30s, when he was walking along his trapline up Slim Creek. He noticed the water had suddenly got dirty and he suspected that perhaps a bear had torn out a beaver dam, so he continued along upstream until he rounded a bend in the creek, and there was a huge herd of caribou crossing. For about half an hour he watched as the herd continued to cross, and from a rough count, he estimated that there were at least 1000 in the herd."

"Ever have any problems with your horses when you were packing?" I asked.

Arne laughed when I asked that question, and then explained, "I was just reminded of the time I took a heavy cookstove far back into the mountains to one of my cabins. It was tied on one of the horses and was so top-heavy that the horse staggered around like a drunken man. At one point, I glanced back to see how the horse was doing and all I could see was four legs sticking up in the air, thrashing violently around. Well, I'm telling you that we had some really tricky work as we tried to untie the stove with the horse's legs lashing out in all directions and the stove almost out of sight in the swamp. It sure took a great amount of effort before we finally managed to cut the horse free and get it back on its feet." Arne summed it all up philosophically by saying, "That was just another day in the life of a big game guide."

Arne impressed upon me how being a guide can give one many lessons in the study of human behaviour and how several weeks or a month in the forest can affect people. "On one trip, I guided a party from Philadelphia back into the mountains for bear. These four fellows were close friends, but before two weeks were out, these men were hardly on speaking terms. Before the trip was finished I had to set up a separate tent for each one of them."

"Any other highlights from your guiding career, Arne?"

"I guess it would be the time I took Mr. Bell of Bell Telephone out on a hunt, he came out with a fine caribou, and I have to say that he was a fine gentleman. Yes! I think that's a real highlight."

"Years ago, I heard you mention a horse you used to own that you were so proud of. Care to talk about that?" I questioned.

"That would be Old Madam, the best horse I ever had. When we left home, she would lead the way into the McGregor and then stop at the first camp. If we were going to the next camp, I would wave her on and she would lead the pack train on to the next camp. She wouldn't get too far ahead, she would always stop and wait. I think she was as good as having another trail hand."

During the winter of 1962/63, I worked in a logging camp in the Torpy Valley just a short distance from Ernest Jensen's cabin. In the evenings I used to walk over to his cabin and pass the time listening to his tales of days gone by. I asked him if he ever trapped bear and he responded by relating the following story.

"I set a bear trap one fall on the remains of a moose. A couple days later I returned to find that the trap and toggle log were gone. I followed the drag trail through a few inches of snow all that day without catching up to it, then returned the next morning and continued the chase. In late afternoon I caught up to it and found a two-year-old, 20 feet up a tree. Somehow it had managed to take the toggle log up with it. Well, that was my only experience with trapping bear as I felt it was just too cruel."

Ernest was just one of several trappers that told me they only used a bear trap once and then put it away for good. I strongly suspect that there are many old rusted out bear traps around or under old tumble-down trappers' cabins.

"I understand that you did a lot more trapping than your brothers. What are some of your memories?" I asked.

"Lots of them. I had a rather funny day when I caught a lynx in my trap. I killed it and put it away in my packsack and then went

Mr. Bell, son of Alexander Graham Bell, with his trophy caribou.

along the trail for a short distance. Well, all of a sudden we had a circus going because that lynx wasn't dead at all. I had a time just getting the sack off my back with it being stretched first one way and then the other. I finally got the pack off and it no sooner hit the ground then the lynx was out the top and back into the woods. Everything happened so fast that I stood there wondering if there ever was a lynx at all or if it was just my imagination." Ernest concluded.

One of the favorite winter treats for these men was an ice-cold apple, and Ernest told me how they would dig a hole under the floor of their cabins and then line it with dry moss and spruce needles. Then they would place the apples in this hole and cover them with an abundant supply of dry moss and needles. This supplied them with fresh fruit for almost the entire winter.

During the summer of 1962, Arne and I spent about a month building heliports in the mountains for the BC Forest Service. Though he was well up in years, he was still strong as a bull and could keep up to anyone. In the evenings after we had finished our day's work, we sat around the campfire and told stories. This went on for a week or so until one evening when he had just finished telling a story. I responded with one about grizzlies, as I had already spent a considerable amount of time watching them around timberline.

After I finished the story, I waited for Arne to come back with another one. Instead, he sat staring into the fire. After a few minutes passed, he finally came back with, "You know, it's a funny thing, some people have had all kinds of experiences in the woods and they're still quite young." Looking back on it, I realize that I brought it on myself. Being that he was over twice as old as I was I should have let him tell more than two stories to each one of mine.

Leaving humour aside, I have to say that it was a real pleasure to know and work with Arne. Along with his brothers he has since passed on, leaving a legacy of admiration and respect among all who knew them.

During one span of 23 years, Arne kept meticulous records of both his fur catch and the prices he received. It is interesting to note the extremes; $165 for a fisher in '28/29, to a low of $5 for two wolverine in '32/33. Also squirrels at three cents in '30/31, and $3.75 for two wolves in '45/46. It must be noted that this was just a small part of his yearly income, as he also guided, ran pack-trains, helped with cattle drives, plus had an assortment of other jobs. He put it quite modestly when he said," I never really hurt for money."

For those who may be interested, this is the total of his trapline take from 1928/29 to 1950/51:

ANIMAL	NUMBER	TOTAL PRICE	AVERAGE PRICE
Fisher	53	$3026.90	$57.11
Squirrel	4796	1058.17	0.22
Weasel	2763	2442.68	0.88
Mink	129	1984.48	15.38
Marten	348	11979.78	34.42
Beaver	365	10893.56	29.84
BOUNTY:			165.00

12

STAN HALE

I WAS 13 YEARS OLD WHEN I FIRST VISITED THE ALPINE, THAT magnificent world of beauty up and around timberline. I remember being surprised to find that someone had taken horses into this remote subalpine valley, even though there were steep mountains all around it. I later learned that this someone was Stan Hale.

Born east of Dome Creek, BC in 1915, Stan first got involved in packing on a small scale with dogs which he later used to great advantage on his trapline. He later learned how to set a pack and tie the diamond hitch from the Jensen brothers, experienced packers.

As a young lad, Stan got a taste of what horse-train packing was all about when his close friend and mentor got involved with a bear. Einar Jensen was travelling through the forest with his horses when the lead horse, which was carrying all the dishes and cookware, met

Outfitter Stan Hale and trail hand Carl Anderson at Slim Lake, 1949.

a bear at close quarters. The horse spooked and ran away into the forest and as it ran, the pack tore open on the underbrush and all the contents spilled out, making a great amount of noise. All this noise only served to spur the horse on to even greater speed and distance with Einar running along behind trying to keep up to the best of his ability. He spent a considerable amount of time searching, but a lot of the supplies were never found.

This was just one of the stories that I remembered Stan telling back in the '40s. Now, 50 years later, he was telling them to me again. I egged him on.

"When I was a young lad many people used to make their own homebrew. Each year during spring breakup a few loggers and several trappers would each have a brew going and they would circulate from one place to the next as each brew became ready, often drinking until the crock was empty. On visiting one of the group for a party, they learned that the occupant was quite distraught because his cat had gone missing a few days earlier and he had no idea what had become of it. As the men proceeded to drink, they would take the ladle, fill their glass and drink up while stories of their winter adventures flew thick and fast." I stopped Stan with a bit of a laugh and then explained to him that this story brought back a few memories, then let him continue. "As the day moved along and the crock level dropped, one gentleman, called the 'Black Swede' because he had real dark hair, went to refill his glass. While he was moving the ladle around, he suddenly came up with the missing cat. He took the cat and fired it out the door, then took the ladle and refilled his glass. They kept right on partying."

"What did you do during the years you had pack trains?" I asked

"Well, I did a whole lot of different things. I used to pack for the Forest Service lookouts and supply camps. There was a little misunderstanding over in Europe so I had to spend five years in the military because of that. After that I got right back into packing again because that was something I knew. That was when I started working with the Army Topographical Surveys and that took me into some pretty remote areas of the province. During those years with the surveys, the shortest trip I took was 110 days and the longest was 140 days."

"How could you carry that much food with you?" I queried.

"We didn't, we had aircraft meet us now and then at a lake that was suitable for them to land on. We also had aircraft make parachute drops to us as needed. Also, I had permission to shoot whatever game was needed for the nutritional health of the crew. It was mostly canned meat that we ate, though."

"How far did you get from home on these surveys?" I asked.

"One of the contracts we had was north of Watson Lake and I sure wasn't going to take my horses that far, so I rented a complete outfit from Skook Davidson who had a whole bunch of horses up on the Big Muddy (Muskwa River). They took us up there by aircraft and I picked up 13 horses and an ugly, bull-headed white mule named Jonathon from him. We worked in there and things went quite well until late fall, and then things went to hell. When fall approached, the muskegs froze over and left us in a hell of a fix. It never froze hard enough to support the weight of the horses so we were unable to move. When we tried to move, the horses would break through and cut their legs and that was the end of that. Finally with winter coming on, we realized we were trapped in there. Then

Dick Corless, renowned riverboat builder and freighter with Skook Davidson at Fort Ware in 1942.

the order came down to destroy the horses and get out to the closest lake where we were to be picked up by an aircraft. Well that's what we did, and the army made it right with Skook for the value of the animals."

"How many horses did you have when you were involved with the surveys?"

"I think the most I ever had was 26, but that was always changing because of buying or selling, or because of accidents."

Stan grimaced as a memory came back. "One of those accidents happened on North Star Mountain just north of the Bowron Lakes, when one of my horses lost its footing and went bouncing down the mountainside. It took me a while to get down to where she was and when I did, I saw that she was split open from end to end. I always carried a .45 colt with me on those trips so I sure didn't let her suffer. Another thing, that horse had a balance problem and never should have been in the mountains at all, but I didn't know it until I was out there.

"I lost another horse by a bit of bad luck. This was just a real freak accident. I had all the horses in a pen up by Pass Lake near the McGregor River when it happened. One of the horses chased a colt along the barbed wire fence and crowded it and almost cut one of its front legs off. I felt like hell but I had to get rid of it."

"Did you ever have any other strange experiences with horses, after all, you certainly spent enough time with them." I suggested.

"Come to think of it, I really did. You know I bought a mare from a rancher in the Peace River district and brought it back to my farm, and a little while later it disappeared. It didn't take me very long to figure out that she had swum the Fraser River, followed the Smoky (Morkill) River back to the height of land, and then found her way all the way back to her home ranch. Horses have a great sense of direction in the forest, you know, if they go somewhere they just never seem to forget it and can go back the same way later on. Well, the next year I brought her back to the farm again and just a short time later she gave birth. I never had any trouble with her leaving after that."

"Is it true that a horse will always go back home if you turn it loose in the forest?" I asked.

"Yes, or to its last good food supply, whichever is closest." Stan answered with a grin.

"I've seen the results of those surveys, Stan, the rock cairns you people placed on those mountain peaks for compass bearings stand out to this day. How far could you go in a day when you were travelling?" I asked.

"When we were travelling through real tough going, say through alder thickets or heavy second growth, we covered as little as three miles. On our best days, about 15 miles. Once we were on location, we would usually travel one day and then set up camp for two days, while the crews did their work. Whenever possible we would travel between five a.m. and two p.m. to avoid overheating the horses in the heat of the day. When we were in the mountains, we tried to travel around timberline as much as possible. It was always easier going up there and a good strong wind would help keep the flies away. The best part of it was that there was always an abundant supply of feed for the horses up there."

"Did you ever get into places where you couldn't get through and had to turn back?" I wanted to know.

"Lots of times we had to change direction because of heavy snow-drifts early in the year, but the worst I ever ran into was along the Goat River where second growth spruce and alder thickets meant many hours of trail cutting. In one area we ran into a very big snow slide that completely blocked our access and it looked like we would have to turn back." Stan paused for a minute and then continued. "I looked the slide over real good and found a place where the spring runoff had undercut the slide to such an extent that it was possible to get the horses through. Man! I'm telling you that gave me the creeps going under there. I knew there was little chance that it would move while I was under it, but was I ever glad to get by it."

"How far was it through the slide?" I asked.

"About 200 feet, I guess, but it seemed a lot more than that." He added.

"You must have had some interesting experiences with animals through all those years, didn't you?"

This brought a chuckle out of Stan as he recalled: "You bet. I remember the time during rutting season when a horny bull moose came tearing into camp and started making passes at the horses. When the smoke and dust cleared, that moose was ready for the stew pot. But we had an even more exciting day the time that a grizzly followed the horses into camp. I fired my 30-30 into the air to try to scare it off, but it wouldn't go. I tried to shoot again but the gun malfunctioned. Finally, I jumped on the back of one of the horses and rode around waving a large pack cover and managed to drive it off.

"The only other time that I was bothered by bear was when a grizzly came into camp while I was away. It ate the toes out of a pair of boots, then ate half a box of dynamite and left. Most of the time the bells on the horses let the animals know that we were coming."

"Any other problems with animals?" I questioned.

"Actually, we had the most problems with porcupines. Especially with colts. They would walk up to the porcupines and try to sniff them, then get a whack across the nose. I spent quite a bit of time pulling those darned quills out. If I didn't have a pair of pliers handy, I would pull them with my teeth. I remember I had one mare that was good for two or three sessions a year with porcupines. Why she kept going back for more, I don't know. Maybe she thought that if she gave them another chance, they would change. I got sick and tired of pulling quills out of her beak.

"Another time," he went on, "I woke up in the middle of the night to find a porcupine eating my slicker and rain pants. It was about half done by then so there was no point in stopping it. I always was more worried about porcupines and skunks than I was about bears. One morning I woke up in my tent to find a skunk's nose about four inches from mine. Boy! Was it ever sniffing me out."

I reminded Stan that I was at Slim Lake early in 1949 when he came through with his pack train headed for Barkerville to meet the army engineers. "I remember that one of the horses took off on you and you lost over one day getting it back. How long did it take to cover the 60 miles as the crow flies between Dome Creek and Barkerville?"

"It took 12 days as I recall. We had a lot of trouble. First that horse took off and we lost over one day when the trail hand went back for it. Then we ran into huge snow drifts in the passes which forced us to detour for miles around. Other times, because it was early in the year, we had to go miles out of our way just to find feed for the horses."

"It strikes me that this was a way of life that required the ultimate in patience. Why did you give it up, Stan?"

"I had to." he responded. "Every time I came home from an extended stay in the forests, all I had to do was hang my pants over the foot of the bed and my wife got pregnant."

In reality, it was the end of an era. New technology, snowmobiles in winter, and more importantly, helicopters began arriving on the scene, and the days of summer-long pack trains came to a close. With it went another colourful chapter in our history.

13

THE GLEASONS

IN 1912 CHRIS AND FRANK GLEASON, ALONG WITH A FRIEND named Jack Carnasky, left Idaho and headed into a life of adventure in a new land. They came through Ashcroft and Quesnel and then by steamer to Fort George. By September they arrived in Fort St. James and spent the next three winters trapping around the Little Salmon River.

Three years later they left the Fort St. James area and headed up the east fork of the McGregor River to what is now Gleason Creek where they built a cabin and spent the winter. The following summer Jack moved into the East Torpy where he built two cabins. Chris and Frank trapped from Eight-Mile Canyon all the way to Jarvis and Kitchy Creeks. In these general areas these men were to stay, trap, and prospect until 1924, spending both the winters and summers in the forest. This was through some of the best fur markets of all time. Mr. Towers, a well known fur trader at that time, gave them one cheque for $5000 and that was for only part of a winter's catch.

In 1968 I went to Dome Creek several times and had lengthy conversations with Jack Carnasky about his wilderness adventures with his fellow trappers and hunters. Jack was glad to relive their cherished memories and I was elated to record them.

"On the north side of the McGregor River," he began, "just a few miles below Jarvis Creek, was a spot we called Moose Mountain. It was named that because a person was virtually guaranteed of getting a moose there. Well, Frank shot a moose there four days before Christmas, I think it was 1916. Three days later he took his pack board and snowshoed back to get some meat. The temperature had been at –30 degrees, so he hadn't bothered to take his rifle along as he felt certain that all the bears were denned. As he neared the moose, he spotted a grizzly eating on it, and at the same time, the grizzly either saw or heard him and charged. From a distance of about 200 yards, the bear attacked with frightening speed. Frank just had enough time to get his snowshoes off and climb a tree before the bear arrived. He spent several hours up in the tree where he came close to suffering severe frostbite in his legs. Finally, the bear slowly wandered away into the bush and Frank came down the tree. He got back to the cabin just when it was getting dark. The next day, Chris and Frank celebrated Christmas by going back to the moose carcass, but the bear had moved away.

"This was just one of two incidents in which we felt that our lives had been saved because of a 'quick release' method of tying on our snowshoes that we had learned from the Indians at Fort St. James: by twisting one's foot around hard to one side, it was instantly released from the snowshoe."

"Did you fellows have many confrontations with bears?" I asked.

"Yes! We were bound to have. They were everywhere in that country, and there was some real big ones. The firearms we carried were not very powerful by today's standards: I had a .32 Winchester,

Chris and Frank Gleason. The pack in the centre contains 64 beaver pelts.

Frank had a 30-30, and Chris carried a .351 self-loading." Jack stopped to gather his thoughts, and then continued, "I can tell you about one October night that I will never forget. I shot a moose on Moose Mountain quite a long way from our cabin and I carried part of the meat back to the cabin. The next day, Frank and I returned to get the fat, as it was a very fat moose. After we cut all the fat off the moose, we loaded it on our pack boards and set off over the mountain for our cabin. Well we didn't allow enough time for that trip, so the next thing you know it started getting dark. We knew we couldn't make the cabin so we decided to camp under some real big spruce trees. We figured the fat might heat, so we took it off the pack boards and spread it out on a big tree that was lying there beside us. We had figured on being back before dark so we had not brought our bug with us. We just got the fat spread out on the tree and it got dark, so we didn't even get a fire going. Well, we just sat there in the dark and I guess it was sometime around midnight that the dogs

Jack Carnaski,
trapper.
c. 1920.

went tearing out into the darkness barking like crazy, and then something came driving them right back to us. It was absolute bedlam. The dogs were snarling and Frank and I were hollering as loud as we could. Frank had his 30-30 with him but we were afraid to shoot in case it was a mother with cubs. We finally caught hold of the dogs and then held them for dear life while that bear stood eating only a few feet from us. From about midnight until about four in the morning, that bear kept eating while we huddled in terror. We could hear it eating and moving right beside us, and I'm telling you that was a long night. When daylight came, we checked and there was not one piece of fat left. We didn't care, though, we were just darned happy to be alive. We knew darned well that we could have been mauled or killed on what was by far the longest night of our lives."

"I've heard that you fellows used to make your own clothes, Jack, is that true?"

"We made our own pants and moccasins sometimes. We used the bark of hemlock trees in a solution that took almost a year to tan. It had to be changed quite often or it would lose its strength. A pair of moccasin-style boots would last about a year and the pants even longer. We used everything possible that nature provided as it was a long way out for supplies. All fat that we took from bears was rendered down and used for cooking. Even moose tallow was used as a candle by heating it first, then pouring it into a shallow tin like a sardine can. A wire was laid across the top of the can and a wick hung over it into the heated tallow. The heat from the burning wick was sufficient to keep the tallow in liquid form as long as the tin was kept near full. We considered bear meat a delicacy and countless times we ate squirrel or whatever else the forests had to offer. We always had set lines placed in streams and this supplied us with an abundance of fish."

"I have heard stories that you men travelled far and wide in the summers." I said.

"During the summer months we used to prospect, and we ranged freely over on to the eastern slopes of the Rockies. It was on one of these trips to the eastern slopes that we saw the strangest sight of all our years in the forests and mountains. It happened one afternoon when we spent several hours on a mountainside watching two mountain sheep, a lamb and its mother, feeding on an adjacent ridge. Suddenly an eagle that had been circling high above the sheep dropped toward them in a high speed dive. Just at the last instant, the lamb saw or sensed the eagle's presence and jumped under the ewe's belly, while at the same instant the ewe reared up and struck the eagle right in the breast with its horns. The eagle glided right by us around the mountain and out of sight, and its breast was covered with blood. We felt certain that it was mortally wounded."

"I want your opinion on something that I ask all woodsmen, Jack, do you feel that the wolf poisoning program was justified?"

"Well, they certainly killed a pile of game. In a trip along the Torpy Mountains one fall, Frank, Chris, and I came upon the carcasses of sixteen moose and one caribou that were killed by wolf packs. In every case only a small amount of flesh had been eaten, usually only the noses, and they could have been eaten by other animals."

Jack shook his head as another memory returned. "I had a thrilling experience one February, I was snowshoeing along my trapline when a large pack of wolves caught up with me, they surrounded me and then set up a deafening chorus of howls. They stayed just out of sight in the timber, and followed me all the way to the next cabin, a distance of about three miles, and they howled continually all the way there. You know, I kind of think that wolves are very good at sensing fear, and maybe they do this as a form of entertainment. Maybe they get a kick out of scaring the hell out of people. If that was their intent, I sure didn't let them down."

"Another thing," he went on, "I think the wolves were the main reason that boar grizzlies stayed out most of the winter in those days. It was the abundance of food. Wolves would kill a moose, eat just a bit of it and then move on, leaving an endless supply of food for the bears. The grizzlies would kill their own moose as well, so they only had to den up to avoid extremely cold temperatures. I remember when I backtracked a grizzly that I found eating on a moose carcass on the river ice. I found its den about one mile from the moose. I then realized that the bear had either heard the wolves kill the moose or else it had smelled the moose, because its tracks led straight as an arrow from the den to the moose carcass. This bear didn't even have a real den, it had just crawled in under some blowdown in an effort to escape a previous cold snap."

"Did you get some real big bears, Jack?"

"We did. We sold quite a few on the fur market. The biggest one we ever got was shot on the first day of February, and the dried hide weighed about 100 lbs. I figured it weighed about 700 to 800 lbs. We only got $50 for that hide, less than we got for small fur."

"Did you fellows get some real scares from these bears?" I asked.

"You bet, and one of them happened to Frank because of a craving we used to get for doughnuts. You know, that was the greatest enjoyment that we had in the forest. When we got a craving for doughnuts, nothing else mattered. This happened on a trip up near timberline when he was hunting blue grouse. He spent several days up there just walking around and enjoying the view and then he got this craving for doughnuts. He made a fire and heated up the fat and made a whole bunch of them. Well, after he ate his fill, he stretched out on the ground and took a snooze because it was a nice warm day. Quite a while later, he heard something banging the cooking pots around so he woke up and there was this grizzly bear eating the doughnuts. He made a flying leap to grab his rifle that was leaning against a tree, and knocked the kettle off the rock it was sitting on. That bear jumped and swatted the kettle a good one and by that time Frank had the rifle and dropped him."

Without any coaxing, Jack went on. "I had a funny thing happen over doughnuts. It was a cold day in late October and I suddenly got the craving. I stopped beside a stream for a feast and after setting everything up, I shaped the doughnuts and placed them on a rock while I waited for the fire to heat up the fat. Well, when the fat got hot enough I put some doughnuts in and got the surprise of my life. The doughnuts had frozen while sitting on the rocks and when I placed them in the hot fat, they exploded, and sent hot fat out of the pot into the fire. The fire flared up and caught the needles of a spruce tree on fire over my head and then the tree flared right to the top and a tremendous shower of needles came down all over the doughnuts, the campfire, and me. Now that was more than any self-respecting trapper could put up with, so I gave it one well-placed kick and sent the whole confounded thing down the mountainside and that was the end of that."

"When you first went into the McGregor area were the grizzlies afraid of your scent?" I questioned.

"Some were, others seemed more puzzled than afraid. Many times we saw where they crossed our paths where we had just walked and they would spend quite a bit of time with their noses on the ground. I don't think they knew what they were supposed to do with us.

"I saw a strange thing one day right from my cabin at the head of Eight-Mile Canyon. A moose had drifted downriver with the high water and got hung up on a sandbar right across from my cabin. Well, when I got up that morning, I saw a black bear trying to pull it out

Frank Gleason, rawboned and strong as a bull. c. 1940.

of the river. The bank was too steep, though, and it couldn't do it. It pulled and jerked for a while and finally got it moving and then it partly climbed up on the moose and together they went around the bend, right into the canyon. Well, I can tell you, that bear must have had some ride."

"Do you think it could have survived?" I asked.

"No! If you took a look at the bottom end of that canyon, you wouldn't ask that."

"You always had dogs, I understand."

"Most of the time. We had a lot of close encounters with bears although we never lost any dogs to them. They were a godsend to us, these dogs. They usually gave us warning when something was around. They often carried up to 40 lbs. each, and I can't say how much their companionship meant to us. Generally, the dogs would not chase any animals unless we ordered them to, and this was a never-ending source of joy to us as well as a great challenge, to see who could train their dog the best, and we put a lot of time into it.

"One of the dogs — it belonged to Chris — was named Iscum. This dog was so smart that he just had to open the door of the cabin and say, 'Where's the moose, Iscum?' and it would lead off on a hunt that almost always produced a moose — often within 15 or 20 minutes."

"I'll bet you sure got close to the dogs back in there." I suggested.

"We sure did. Most people don't realize just how close you can get to a dog when you spend all your time with it. I can tell you about the time that Chris and Frank were walking along the bank of the McGregor River with their dogs when a startled cow moose with a newborn calf jumped up right in front of them. The noise of the river had prevented the moose from hearing them until they were right upon it. Well, in an effort to protect the men, Iscum jumped and grabbed the moose by the nose. The moose swung its head from side to side a few times in an effort to dislodge the dog, then lowered its head to the ground and struck it a blow with each front foot. Iscum whined and let go, rolled to the side, and then jumped over the bank into the river. As the moose led its calf away, Iscum swam back to shore, climbed up on the bank and died.

"I was at the cabin when they came back and you would think they had just lost a member of their family, the way they carried on. Chris never had a dog like that again, heck! None of us did."

"Was that the only dog that you fellows lost to animals?" I asked.

"Yes, although we lost several in the river. They would run out on the thin ice and break through and get pulled under by the strong current. Dogs can't seem to understand that."

"What are some of your other memories from those days, Jack?" I asked.

"One of our favorite pastimes was to watch animals in spring. We spent many hours in spring watching grizzlies, wolverines, and porcupines on the snow slides. Many times we found where grizzlies had slid down the mountains in the snow. This was definitely a form of entertainment, for sometimes they would climb back up to slide again and again. Once we found a spot where a grizzly had slid all the way from the alpine down to the river flats, a distance of over one mile. At one point the mountain dropped off to nearly vertical for a distance of several hundred feet, which means that the bear had to be travelling at tremendous speed when it reached the bottom of the steep part. That bear didn't climb back up for a second run.

"Another time Frank and I watched a mother grizzly with two cubs as they wandered across a mountain just a short way below timberline. Every now and then a cub would run up and bite the mother on her heel. Whirling around, the mother would chase them for a few hundred feet, then continue on her way. No sooner would she get started, then one of the cubs would run and bite her again. We watched them play like that for about an hour, until they disappeared from view.

"We had lots of animals to watch in the winter." Jack continued, "When the ice on the river was frozen solid and windswept, it made for ideal walking conditions and was the 'highway of the wilderness,' not only for us men, but for all the wildlife in the area. Many times we were forced to leave the river ice and walk around angry moose that would rather fight than go out into the crusted snow which cut their legs.

"When we were using the river in this manner, we would cut poles and tap the ice ahead of us. If the pole didn't break through, then the ice would most certainly support us on snowshoes. I recall the time I neglected to test the ice and almost died because of it." Jack told me. "That took place when I left my cabin just above Eight-Mile Canyon one morning and went along the trail until I hit Garden Creek. I crossed on a foot-log and made a big circle through the forest to look over some new area for trapping. When I hit the creek again I was about half a mile below the foot-log, so rather than walk back, I decided to cross on the ice which looked safe. Right in the middle of the creek was a patch of ice with snow on it, and I no sooner touched it than I found myself in the water up to my neck. I got my hands on solid ice, but found that I could not get out because the strong current was pulling against my snowshoes. I held on with one hand, grabbed one snowshoe under the ice, and twisted it hard to one side. This released it because of the special way it was tied. I then did the same with the other snowshoe and managed to climb out on the ice. Quick as I could, I got waterproof matches and birch bark out of my pack and got a roaring fire going against a big dry snag. Then I found that I was getting colder because the wind was blowing the heat away. I knew that I was in trouble so I made a run for the cabin and was at the point of collapse when I arrived at the door. The cabin was still warm from the morning fire so a little later on I was able to remove my pants, socks, and moccasins, which had frozen solid by the time I reached the cabin. Another thing I have to say is that this was the second time we got out of bad trouble because of the way of tying our snowshoes that the Indians showed us."

"Did you men ever get lost in the forest, Jack?"

"Not really lost. You have to be pretty careless to get lost in the mountains, especially if it's not cloudy. I did have some fun one day, though, when I set out on my snowshoes to blaze a new line and set traps. It was snowing when I left the cabin and it continued as I did my work. In the afternoon, I was just going to turn back when I came upon a fresh snowshoe trail. I followed it very carefully, wondering who would have the nerve to trap on my line. As I moved along, I came upon a fresh trap set and realized it was my own. I had gone in a complete circle and was only a 15-minute walk from my cabin. The next morning I set out again, picked up the traps and ran a new line, but that time I used my compass."

"Did you ever have any problem with people stealing your fur?" I asked.

"No! We used to store our fur in a cabin in the pass, and sometimes we had thousands of dollars worth of furs in there. We hardly ever stayed there, but we never had any trouble."

"If you were to leave those furs there today, they would probably go missing during the first week, don't you think?" I asked.

"No! I don't agree. I think the furs would still be safe today if the penalty for stealing it was still the same." Then with a steely glint in his eyes, Jack added, "You know, in those days if you got caught — you got shot."

The last time that I visited Jack at his home in Dome Creek, I asked him about Chris and he told me that he hadn't heard from him for about four years. As he was about 80 years old at that time, Jack figured that he had probably passed on. Since Frank had passed away in the '50s, I felt that Jack was my only chance to get the stories of their great adventures so many years before.

In 1976 I was visiting a mountain-climbing friend named Bill Benedict in Vancouver when the thought occurred to me to check the White Rock phone book, as that was where Chris had lived when Jack last heard from him. I found a Chris Gleason listed so I called the number, hoping it was the same man. When a woman answered the phone, I immediately assumed I had the wrong person. I asked if I could speak to Chris and she answered, "Just a minute."

Then a man answered and I asked, "Is this the same Chris Gleason that used to trap the McGregor Plateau 60 years ago?"

"It sure is!" came the response. After a few more words were spoken, Bill and I drove out to White Rock to visit, and we quickly realized why Chris had quit writing to Jack. He had met a lady and tied the knot, and not wanting Jack to think he had taken leave of his senses, had quit writing to him.

Eighty-two-years-young and in obviously failing health, he was delighted to reminisce about his years in the mountains. He had nothing but smiles when he remembered their many encounters with grizzlies, and he had nothing but scorn for the efforts being made at that time to glorify wolves as predators that take only the sick and weak. He pointed out that countless times they found their kills, animals of all sizes and ages, often with only a few pounds of flesh eaten, while the packs moved on to kill again and again.

One of his wolf-related exploits was recorded in the Prince George *Citizen* on February 16, 1933:

C. Gleason Brings down
Timber Wolf at Dome Creek

Dome Creek, Feb. 10 — Chris Gleason brought down a big timber wolf on Wednesday in the vicinity of the Dome Creek school. He came across the tracks while walking past the school and they indicated the animal had been hanging around for some time. Getting his snowshoes and rifle, Gleason picked up the tracks and after stalking the animal, brought it down with a well placed shot. It measured 6 feet, 6 inches from tip to tip. The incident has caused no little excitement in Dome Creek, as while living close to nature the parents of the children do not relish wolves hanging around in the bush fringing the school house. They are considering the election of a sniper, and Chris Gleason is in line for the job.

Wolves have been numerous around Dome Creek this winter, day and night the cry of the packs may be heard. Last week Ernest Jensen shot a large wolf on the Fraser opposite his dwelling, and Skook Davidson on visiting his trapping grounds came upon the carcass of a deer on the ice just a short distance from Dome Creek, which apparently had been killed by wolves.

The settlers are also getting anxious about their stock when it is turned loose in the spring. With so many on the relief list they think the government could kill two birds with one stone by offering a substantial bounty on the wolves, as this would start a number of men after the wolves, protect the settlers stock and the game, and take the hunters off the relief lists.

CHRIS WENT OUT OF HIS WAY TO TRY TO MAKE ME UNDERSTAND that he didn't hate wolves. He seemed to echo other trappers verbatim when he said that he loved the call of the wolf packs but that the slaughter was completely out of hand. During the course of our conversation, Chris touched on a subject that had been whispered about for most of my lifetime: the disappearance of a trapper named Goodson from the Torpy River area around what is now called Goodson Creek, a tributary of Walker Creek which runs into the Torpy about seven miles northeast of Dome Creek.

Another trapper that worked the Torpy-Pass Lake area was a man named E. B. Shorty Haynes, and these two men had one thing in common: they didn't like each other.

The arrival of E. B. Haynes into this area was carried in the *Fort George Tribune* dated November 13, 1909:

Bear River Trapper Reported Drowned

Late last spring Jack Dawson and E. B. Haynes left Barkerville intending to go north to Fox River, a tributary of the [illegible] to engage in trapping. They crossed to Bear Lake and went down the Bear River. En route they met parties from the north who told them that two outfits were then on Fox River and others intended to go there. This information made them change their plans, and they decided to return to Bear River to trap on it this winter. They returned and established camps, their upper camp being at a point about 35 miles from the mouth of the river. Of late they have been making preparations to cut trails on which to set a line of traps. On Saturday morning, November 6th, Dawson left the cabin to go downstream to engage at the work, while Haynes went upstream. They had a canoe a mile below the cabin, and Dawson was to take it and go on down to where they had a tent and a boat, some seven or eight miles, where they intended to build a winter covering for the boat and canoe. On returning to the cabin on Saturday evening, Haynes did not find Dawson there, as he expected; a dog that had gone with him was there. He fired several shots, but got no answer. He went down to where the canoe had been tied; but there were no signs there. It was then too late to make further search and he returned to the cabin. Early Sunday morning Haynes resumed the search. He went down the river to the tent and boat, but saw no trace of Dawson or the canoe. He came to the conclusion that Dawson was drowned, the river being obstructed in places by log jams and sweepers, which are dangerous if care is not exercised in passing them. Haynes searched down the river to the Fraser and came on to Fort George, where he arrived on Tuesday night. He reported the facts to James Cowie, manager of the Hudson's Bay Company store, who is a Justice of the Peace. On Thursday morning, Haynes, accompanied by Bob Alexander and Frank Seymour, started over the trail for Bear River, a three-day trip. Dawson lived at Van Winkle seven years, was an Englishman, and 43 years of age.

∽

THE BEAR (BOWRON) RIVER WAS FROZEN OVER BY THE TIME the men got there, so the search was not undertaken. Dawson's body was never found. William Goodson and Shorty Haynes, who stood 6 feet, 6 inches, both served in the war. Shorty was employed as a sniper by the 102nd for two years. Sometime after November 12th, 1926, Goodson disappeared. *The Citizen* carried the story in its March 11th, 1926 edition:

Police Search for Missing Dome Creek Trapper
William Allan Goodson Has Been
Missing From His Trapline Since November 12th
Writing Found in His Cabin Which
Dealt With Fight With E. B. Haynes

Sergeant Walker, of the provincial police, has instituted a search for William Allan Goodson, a trapper who has made Dome Creek his headquarters for a number of years. The initial move in the search was entrusted to Constable Sam Service of McBride. Upon a visit to Dome Creek he ascertained that Goodson made a trip out from his trapline to Dome Creek on October 14th for the purchase of supplies. Goodson at this time left a letter with James Stewart, postmaster, with instructions that he turn the same over to the police upon the next visit to Dome Creek of any member of the force. There was no police visit and Stewart was holding the letter when Goodson returned on November 2nd for further supplies. He made inquiries about the letter he had left with Stewart and asked for its return. It happened the letter had been misplaced and Stewart was unable to return it. Goodson got the supplies he wanted and started back for his trapline, situated at the junction of the Torpy and Clearwater Rivers, about 12 miles from McBride. So far as Stewart could remember Goodson appeared to be in good health. His visit to Dome Creek is the last record of his having been seen.

On February 26th, in company with E. B. Haynes and another resident, Constable Service started on a trip to the Goodson cabin, which was reached next day. It was found to be in good condition, and there was no evidence of a struggle. The dishes had been washed and put away. There was no fur in the cabin, neither was there any tobacco, and the inference was that Goodson had left the cabin to secure further supplies.

Among the papers found in the cabin was a voluminous writing in the nature of a journal, which was commenced on October 4th and continued with a few breaks down to November 12th. The subject matter related to a fight which Goodson said he had with E. B. Haynes, in the course of which he alleged he had been hit with a hammer. From his writings one would gather that for a time he feared his injuries would prove fatal, but he appeared to be going strong when he visited Dome Creek on November 2nd, although upon his return to the cabin he resumed his writing and kept it going until November 12th.

So much snow had fallen that it was impossible for Constable Service to track Goodson from his cabin. In cruising around in the bush before reaching the cabin the constable and E. B. Haynes came upon a rifle suspended in a tree, which Haynes said belonged to Goodson. The circumstance that Goodson was known to carry a pistol while in the bush was offered as an explanation for his leaving the rifle in a tree.

E. B. Haynes is said to admit having a quarrel with Goodson some time ago, but contends it did not amount to anything, and he denies that a hammer or any other kind of weapon was used. The police inquiry is to be carried further with a view to locating Goodson. He carried a substantial balance in one of the Prince

George banks and made no withdrawals from his account since September last.

The missing man was well known in McBride and vicinity. He was 58 years old, stood 6 feet, 2 inches and weighed 190 pounds. He saw service in the world war and up to August last was in receipt of a monthly pension of $15 on account of injuries received. This pension was cut off after August, following a medical examination, when Goodson's condition was found to be normal. From letters found in his cabin Goodson is believed to have a wife, Mrs. Mabel Goodson of Columbus, Ohio, and a son, L.W. Goodson of Newark, Ohio.

NO TRACE OF GOODSON WAS EVER FOUND. BUT NOW CHRIS informed us that he had known something about this case all through the years and that he wanted to tell it because as he put it, "all the others are dead and it will just die with me, so I might as well tell you."

"Shorty and Goodson had trouble going back to the war, and things didn't get any better. One day Shorty came to my brother Frank and said, 'Goodson burned one of my cabins down and I'm going to kill him for it.' Well, Goodson was never seen after that.

"Another thing, Shorty and Goodson got into a terrible fight at a house near Kidd, and Goodson was carried from the house unconscious. Shorty was nobody to fool around with. He was the kind of man who boiled up slow, but when he did, he boiled up mighty hot."

"My dad used to say that Shorty was a Texas Ranger before he came to Canada. Do you know anything about that, Chris?"

"He never told me that, but I know that he was a dead shot with both a rifle and handgun."

"My dad said that he could pick off mice in the cabin with the pistol lying across his chest."

"Well, I believe that all right. But I'm telling you that I knew Shorty for a long time and he was a good man and a just man."

After Chris made that statement, he became silent and I knew that the discussion about Goodson and Haynes was over. I couldn't help but feel that at the very least there had been a conspiracy of silence, and that there was still much left unsaid. In fact, a line from Robert Service's *Cremation of Sam McGee* came to mind: "…and the trail has its own stern code."

When the subject of Skook Davidson came up, Chris showed great interest. He informed us that Skook was the only man that ever took Frank in a wrestling match. Frank, who ran the general store in Dome Creek and later the post office when it was reopened, was a powerful raw-boned man who used to carry 45-gallon drums of kerosene on his shoulder from the railroad station to his store, a distance of about 100 feet.

"I'd sure like to hear about some of your experiences with bears, Chris, you must have had a few of them." I suggested, hoping to get him going.

*E. B.
'Shorty' Haynes.
c. 1945.*

"We had lots of them. I think Frank would have been a good one to ask about that because he had quite a few of them. He sure got a surprise one day when he was fishing the Torpy. The salmon were running so you know the bears were there. Well, Frank had a bear come out of the bush and give him a slap in the back, and before he knew it, the bear was back in the bushes again. Well, Frank got the message and got the hell out of there in a hurry."

"How did the grizzlies react to your presence when you first went into that country?" I asked.

"They didn't seem very impressed by human scent in those days. Often they would walk around quite close to where we camped, and they stayed in the general area of our cabins. We would see their tracks quite often."

"Jack told me about your dog, Iscum. That must have been quite a loss."

"Yes. I sure could have used him the next year when I got into trouble. I was trapping muskrats up Jarvis Creek in the spring when I had some fun with a grizzly. I had skinned out about 150 rats and thrown them in a pile about 200 feet from the small tent I was camping in. One evening I returned to the tent to find that a grizzly had walked in through one wall and out through the other. As there was no sign of the bear, I patched the tent as best I could and then retired for the night. Just before dark, I heard a noise right beside my head and realized it was the grizzly. With cold shivers running up and down my spine, I just kind of froze and remained motionless as the grizzly stuck its nose through the torn tent and touched my cheek. It sniffed several times and then pulled its head out of the tent and walked over to where the rats were piled and began feeding. I was really shook up, so I got my gun and shot that bugger before he decided to come back."

"Don't you think that you brought the bear to you by piling up those rat carcasses?" I questioned.

"No! I don't think it made any difference because I had the fur with me and the scent was all over everything. I'll tell you one thing though, I made up my mind that I would never be in the woods without a dog again. Especially tent camping."

"Any other experiences with bears?" I asked.

"Many. There was the time, that was in October, when I was walking along the river and I saw this grizzly bear across the river. It was upstream from me so I started walking to get closer for a shot, because we sure needed some bear for food and fat. As I moved quietly along, that bear suddenly waded out into the water and began swimming across. Well, I was sure surprised, so I hid behind some brush and waited. You know, the current brought the bear downriver and it came out on the bank only 20 feet from me. By this time my heart was pounding so much that I could hardly steady the gun. Well, I fired a shot, and the bear let out a big 'woof' and jumped into cover. I listened but I couldn't hear it running away. I sat still for at least half an hour to give it time to die, and then I slowly moved in, following the blood trail. You know, I only took a few steps and that bear tore out of the thicket straight at me. I guess I just responded on instinct and

A Skook Davidson pack train. c. 1940.

fired three shots from my .351. One of the shots hit it low in the neck and it dropped right beside me. I'm telling you I was shaking so much that I had to wait half an hour before I was able to skin it out."

Chris shook his head a few times for emphasis, then went on. "After that scare, I decided that there had to be a safer way to get bear, so I took my big bear trap with its 16 inch jaws and set it on the remains of a wolf-killed moose carcass that a grizzly had adopted. A couple of days later, I went to check the trap and found I had caught a three year old grizzly. Right away I noticed that the bear was badly rubbed on one side, so I knew the hide would be worthless. I took a few pictures of the bear in the trap, and then decided to try releasing it. The bear was caught by a front pad, so I cut a pole about 15 feet long, and then tied my knife on the end of it. I slowly worked myself into position and began to cut at the bears wrist. At first it fussed a little, then it settled down and didn't move until I was finished. As soon as I saw that the bear was free, I grabbed my rifle, but I didn't need it. That bear was so exhausted from fighting the trap that it got up and slowly wandered away into the woods. You know, several times in later years we ran into this bear's tracks, and they sure were strange tracks."

"Were you always worried about injuries back in there?" I asked.

"We sure were. You knew that if you got hurt bad that you would die, so we did our best to be careful. I want to tell you fellows about an experience I had with traps. After I had that bad scare from the grizzly, I decided it would be safer to trap them, so I set the bear trap on a moose carcass that a grizzly had taken from the wolves. Well, I set it right on the bear's trail and covered it lightly so the bear couldn't see it. After I finished the job, I gathered up my pack and rifle, and started along the path back to the cabin. Well, I only took a few steps and was about to put my foot right on the trap, when I remembered. Instantly, I threw myself to the side, then sat there on the ground shaking uncontrollably for a while. I knew very well that if I had stepped in the trap, it would have meant an agonizing death in that remote wilderness. Before I got up off the ground, I took a stick and sprung the trap, then took it back to the cabin, and it was never used again."

"Jack told me that you men never lost any dogs to bear, is that correct?" I asked.

"Oh! We had some brushes with bears, but the dogs usually obeyed us when we told them to lie down. I remember one morning when we were all sleeping in the cabin and one of the dogs started yelping something awful. We got out of bed as fast as we could because we figured an animal was killing it. Well, when we got dressed and got outside, here was this poor dog dragging our axe around the cabin. Frank had shot a moose a few days earlier and we had cut it up. Then it went to 30 below and when the dog licked the axe blade its tongue froze there instantly. By the time we warmed up some water to pour on the axe, that poor dog had torn free. It sure suffered for a time there."

Chris laughed as one recollection came back to him: "It was around the end of September and Frank and I were hunting blue grouse up near timberline. We were going through those patches of trees when all of a sudden a cow caribou came tearing out on the run. We stood with our guns at the ready, expecting a grizzly or a pack of wolves to come out, instead, out came a bull moose, grunting continually. The caribou ran by only 100 feet from us, and when the moose went by, it hardly gave us a glance. We spotted them again going through a meadow close to a mile away, and the caribou had established a sizable lead. Those bulls go kind of crazy when they're mating, so you know what he was after."

"There used to be an old prospector that lived on the Torpy. I think he was called Old Samson. Did you know him, Chris?"

"Yes. We used to stop and talk with him whenever we went by. He lived about 10 miles up from the Forks. Used to prospect all over the country. When we stopped there, we would always holler from a ways off because he had a dog that was as wild as the wolves it howled back at. Well, he would come out and ask us if we had any milk, and then he would ask if there were any wars going on. After that, he would head back to his cabin again. Well, in the spring of '21, Frank and I were going by his place so we hollered several times and he never came out. Then the dog came snarling at us and it was in terrible condition. We knew something was wrong so we shot the dog and then went to the cabin, but we couldn't get in because it was locked from the inside." Chris paused for a minute and then continued, "We walked out to Dome Creek and called the police, and the next day Constable Service and Van Dyke, the game warden, went up there and broke the door down. He had lived there since 1913, and the police said that he was 68 years old, so that meant he was born in Sweden about 1853. He was a pioneer, that's for sure. Well, they found him dead in his bunk, so they buried him in his little garden alongside the cabin. They put a cross on his grave with his name on it, and I think it said: Swen Sansen — born in Sweden — 1853–1921, or something like that."

"Did you have some funny times, too?"

"One comes to mind. It was just before dark one winter day when Frank and I came to one of our line cabins that we hadn't visited for a while. When we opened the door, there was a skunk under the bunk peering up at us. After giving it a bit of thought, we tied a # 0 trap to a long pole, and then while Frank held the dogs, I moved the trap ever so slowly over to the skunk. Very carefully I backed the skunk into a corner until it placed one foot against the pan of the trap and got caught. It caught the skunk's foot, but not hard enough to really hurt it. Then I backed out the door ever so slowly, leading the skunk away from the cabin. Everything went fine until I got about 50 feet from the cabin, then, and I don't know why, maybe everything was going too slow for them, anyway, the dogs broke free from Frank and then it was every man for himself. While the dogs were tearing the skunk apart, we ran and hid in the cabin. Then we watched as the dogs killed the skunk and spent a great deal of time rolling over and over in the snow trying to get rid of the stink. Man's best friends? Not that winter. They spent a great deal of time outdoors.

"I've got one more story that you might get a kick out of. This happened after we came out of the mountains. Frank and I decided to have Jack over for Christmas dinner, so we roasted a big goose for the occasion. After it was cooked, we put it outside to cool, while we had a few drinks to get into the spirit of things. Well, when it came time to eat, we went out to get the goose and it was gone, and the roaster was gone, too. Well, Frank got upset and he went into great detail about what he was going to do to that S O B who took the goose. Well, we ate what was left and got by, and when Jack went back home that evening the mystery was solved. There on the stand by his house was the empty roaster, and beside it lay his dog, all stretched out with a satisfied look on its face. A quick check showed that the roaster was empty. Well, we sure got a kick out of that, and whenever Frank saw Jack's dog after that he used to point at it and tell it that it was living on borrowed time."

"Any more memories of humorous events?" I wanted to know.

"One that I like. I came out of the mountains to Dome Creek for supplies, I think it was back about 1920. While I was out, I stopped at old Hooker's and he showed me a radio. Well, I couldn't believe it. When I got back in the mountains again I told Frank and Jack that this little box could hear a man talking all the way from New York. Well, you should have heard them laugh, you'd think it was the funniest thing that they had ever heard. I didn't know how to explain it, so the more I said, the worse it got. By the time they got done with me, I was laughing just as much as they were."

As the time was passing quickly, and Chris was obviously tiring, I threw in a few quick questions.

"Did you men use dugouts back in there?"

"We built about seven dugouts out of cottonwood trees. They're best, you know. We took those dugouts from the McGregor right through to Pass Lake by cutting all the windfalls (down trees) out of Pass Creek. I'm telling you that Pass Lake was just loaded with big Dolly Varden in those days. The smallest ones were about five pounds. Well, after we had our fill of Pass Lake, we went down the Torpy River and then back up Goodson Creek and back to the McGregor again."

"How long did it take to make the round trip?" I asked.

"We weren't in a hurry, I'd say close to a month."

"What was your favorite place in that whole area?"

"I'd say from Jarvis Creek up around that big mountain that they call Alexander now. That was called Sitzi in those days. I looked on the map a few years back and I was surprised that it wasn't Sitzi any-more. We used to spend quite a bit of time around there in the summers, you know."

"Were you men sick very much back in there? I mean you couldn't have had a completely nutritious diet."

"That's a funny thing. We only caught colds when we came out to civilization, and they would go away in a few days when we got back to the forests."

"Any comments about wolverines, Chris."

"Just that they can cause a trapper an awful lot of grief. If they start following your line and eating up your fur, then you have to get them or they'll break you. If they ever become trap-wise, they can follow a trapline for years rendering the fur valueless by tearing it up or eating it. A smart wolverine will turn the trap over and spring it, and then steal the bait. Some trappers caught them by setting their traps upside down."

Jarvis Lake with Alexander (Sitzi) Mountain in the background.

At one point during our conversation I asked Chris, "If you were a young man and had it to do over, would you spend those years in the wilderness?"

After a few seconds, he softly answered, "No, there's too much loneliness, I'd never do that again."

After we had talked for several hours, Chris lapsed into a long period of reflective silence and I sensed that he was no longer in the room with us.

He had gone back.

Back to the forests and mountains.

Back to where all the loneliness of a thousand nights around camp-fires is expressed so eloquently by the mournful howl of wolf packs echoing among moonlit mountain peaks.

Far back along a frozen river where a snowshoe trail winds through the forest to a tiny cabin nestled among the trees. There is a light in the window of the cabin, and by the dim light of a moose-tallow candle a young trapper skins and stretches his daily catch of fur.

He is a young man once again silently paddling his dugout canoe along Jarvis Creek, as the soul-stirring call of a loon drifts down the restless mountain air and moose stare in wonder as he glides swiftly by.

At last we rose to leave and after walking us to the door and bidding us goodbye, Chris added, almost as an afterthought, "You know I've lived in the city for a long time now and yet it's a funny thing: I dream a lot, in fact I dream every night, and in all my dreams I see mountains and rivers."

As we walked away, I thought of Chris, Frank, Ole, Arne and all the other woodsmen of their time, who gave and endured so much. I found myself wishing with all my heart that they will always dream of mountains and rivers. And may God grant that their mountains are rugged and lofty, with goat and sheep on their skylines, eagles riding the updrafts, and grizzlies forever working the slides that stretch down to clear peaceful rivers teeming with fine trout.

APPENDIX 1

Prior to the construction of the grand Trunk Pacific Railroad, the waterways were the main means of transportation. The distances between points along these rivers were published in the *Fort George Herald* on April 13, 1911:

Distances from Fort George

Fort George is central for a large area of country, the greater part of which is suitable for farming. It is located near the geographical centre of the province and at the junction of two rivers, which are navigable for steamboats for 675 miles. Going east and southeast, following the Fraser River upstream, are the following points

	Miles from Fort George
Goose Country Ranch	16
Mouth of Little Salmon	22
Mouth of Willow River	25
Giscome Portage	41
Thomas Cabin	61
Mouth of Big Salmon River	68
Mouth of Bear (Bowron) River	81
Mouth of Tonequah Creek	95
Head of Grand Canyon	106
Slim Creek	139
Dome Creek	156
Clearwater River	164
Smoky River	188
Goat River	201
Garnet Creek	214
Snowshoe Rapids	218
Moose Rapids	220
Beaver River	257
Shuswap River	264
Tête Jaune Cache *(via surveyed line Grand Trunk Pacific, 206)*	315
Edmonton, Alberta *(via surveyed Grand Trunk Pacific (est.))*	461

At Giscome Portage, a wagon road of eight miles connects the Fraser River with Summit Lake, and Summit Lake is the source or head of the Parsnip River, which is the south fork of the Peace River, Finlay River being the north fork, and from their junction the river is called the Peace. Summit Lake is on the Arctic slope or watershed, for the waters of Peace River flow into the Arctic Ocean. The distances to the following points via Giscome Portage are:

Miles from Fort George

Summit Lake	49
Fort McLeod on McLeod Lake	116
Mouth of Parsnip River	196
Fort Grahame on Finlay River	261
Ingenika Mines on McDonnell Creek	360
Fort St. John on Peace River	360

Going west and northwest and upstream on the Nechako and Stuart Rivers the distances are:

Indian Rancherie No. 3	11
Mud River	20
Mouth of Stuart River	57
Mouth of Stoney Creek	
(via Stoney Creek Trail 75 miles)	90
Fort Fraser on Fraser Lake	
(via Stoney Creek Trail 101 miles)	120
Burns Lake on Telegraph Line Trail	156
Aldermere in Bulkley Valley	237
Hazelton at head of navigation	
on Skeena River	297
Prince Rupert on Pacific Ocean	459

South via Fraser River and the Cariboo Road are the following places:

Fort George Canyon	15
Hixon Creek Trail	45
Mouth of Blackwater River	60

Cottonwood Canyon 75
Quesnel
   (Barkerville is 60 miles east of Quesnel) 95
Soda Creek
   (lower end of steamboat navigation) 155
150 Mile House on Cariboo Wagon Road 183
83 Mile House on Cariboo Wagon Road 250
Clinton 285
Ashcroft on Canadian Pacific Railway 230
Vancouver on the Strait of Georgia 524

There are feeding places on the road between Fort George and Quesnel as follows: Long Meadow 21 miles, Round Meadow 38 miles, Swan Creek 61, Goose Lake 85, Quesnel 110 miles. Blackwater Crossing is on this road, 60 miles from Fort George. A trail runs east from Fort George to Bear (Bowron) River, 40 miles

APPENDIX 2

The following is a copy of a typical letter from fur buyer to trapper:

TR inity 6390

510 **W. HASTINGS**
Opposite Spencer's

R. C. TOWERS
RAW AND DRESSED
FUR DEALER
★
OFFICE: B-5 Standard Bank Bldg.

VANCOUVER, B.C.   Mar.21/40

A.Jensen
Dome Creek B.C.

These Marten are very springy.
It will need a lot of Hair Vigor on their
napes to keep them from going bald altogether,
when they go in to the dressers. The one is
nearly gone down to the waist. However I sup
pose that is not the Martens fault. He likely
did the best he knew how.

Beaver are still very high although they
are declining a little every week. I still can
not guarantee a price on them.All I can do is
allow the price of the day they come in and
then pray that I can sell right away. It wont
do much good to get sore and bite me for these
prices,as I know you cant bite very hard now
with those iron teeth.

I got your last wire okay on Saturday.It
was late but came through that day.

Even Squirrels you know get springy.They
dont show on the leather,but after they are
dressed they are singed so that they look
very tough,and they dont have the gloss that
the winter ones have.

With regards and best wishes
yours truly

R.C.Towers

INDEX